He
Cutteth
Out
Rivers

Preparing For the Flow of
God's POWER In Your Life

EBED
PUBLICATIONS

In love, serve one another

by

Dr. John Polis

He Cutteth Out Rivers
Copyright © 1997 — Dr. John Polis

All Scripture references are from the Authorized King James Version of the Bible, unless otherwise marked.

References marked NIV are from the New International Version of the Bible, © copyright 1973, 1978, 1984 by International Bible Society, Colorado Springs, Colorado.

EBED Publications is a division of
The McDougal Publishing Company,
Hagerstown, Maryland.

Published by:

ƐBƐD Publications
P.O. Box 3595
Hagerstown, MD 21742-3595

ISBN 1-884369-50-2

ACKNOWLEDGMENTS

An undertaking as great as writing a book is more of a team effort than an individual accomplishment, and appreciation is due to many who were involved in transferring the message from the heart of the messenger to this written form which has the potential of being distributed to many more people. I would like to say a special thanks to John Carnes, Ashleigh Andrews, Frank Bilotta and Becky Teets, all members of the office staff at our home church in Fairmont, West Virginia, for their continued support in my bookwriting efforts and for volunteering their time to prepare the drafts. A special thanks goes to Pam Freed who typed the final draft before it went to the publisher. God bless you all.

Most of all, I am grateful to the Holy Spirit for revealing His truths to my heart over a period of years. It is those truths which make up the contents of the book.

He cutteth out rivers among the rocks ... .

Job 28:10

CONTENTS

Afterward he brought me again unto the door of the house; and, behold, waters issued out from under the threshold of the house eastward: for the forefront of the house stood toward the east, and the waters came down from under from the right side of the house, at the south side of the altar. Then brought he me out of the way of the gate northward, and led me about the way without unto the utter gate by the way that looketh eastward; and, behold, there ran out waters on the right side.

And when the man that had the line in his hand went forth eastward, he measured a thousand cubits, and he brought me through the waters; the waters were TO THE ANKLES. Again he measured a thousand, and brought me through the waters; the waters were TO THE KNEES. Again he measured a thousand, and brought me through; the waters were TO THE LOINS. Afterward he measured a thousand; and it was a river that I could not pass over: for the waters were risen, waters TO SWIM IN, a river that could not be passed over. Ezekiel 47:1-5

FOREWORD

I have known Dr. John Polis for some years now and consider him to be one of the hardest working men I know in the Body of Christ. Despite the fact that he is the shepherd of two great churches, he still finds the time to minister to others, both nationally and internationally.

I therefore count it a privilege to recommend this book, which I have found to be both scholarly and deeply spiritual, to all those who are hungering for the deeper things of God. It is intriguing and exciting and, at the same time, will guide the reader into new levels of spiritual anointing. It is a word "in due season" and one to be savored.

Rev. David P. Crank
Faith Christian Ministries Church
Fenton, Missouri

INTRODUCTION

He that believeth on me, as the scripture hath said, out of his belly shall flow rivers of living water. (But this spake he of the Spirit, which they that believe on him should receive: for the Holy Ghost was not yet given; because that Jesus was not yet glorified.)   John 7:37-39

God's desire is to use each of His children to bless others around them. In this way, we become extensions of His hands, part of His river of life-giving water that blesses anyone it touches. What a privilege this is!

Blessing others, however, does not happen automatically. Before we can pour forth God's blessing to others, our heavenly Father has to do a work in us, a preparation for His anointing that will rest upon us and become so strong that it will overflow onto others.

As part of this preparation, through a sovereign work of His Spirit, God slowly but surely creates in us a channel through which His blessings can flow to others. We are like rock through which a channel must be cut.

There is a process involved in this cutting that God does in us, a process that some find unpleasant. Just as a natural river cuts its way across the landscape, widening and deepening itself as it goes, until it becomes a mighty rushing stream, God's Spirit is at work in our lives, deepening and widening our ability to receive Him and, therefore, to pour forth His goodness to others.

This process begins small at first. The initial stages of the Spirit's work in us may not seem remarkable at all, but God knows what He is doing, and if we continue in Him, He will cut ever deeper, and the flow of blessing in us, and thus through us, will steadily grow, as well.

The process begins with the very first levels of anointing that we experience and continues with every touch of God that we subsequently receive. With every touch, the Master is carving out His channels of blessing in us.

As you read the pages of this book, I pray that you may allow God to carve out His channels of blessing in you, as well and that you may be challenged to move from one level of anointing to another until you find *"waters to swim in."*

Dr. John Polis
Fairmont, West Virginia

CHAPTER ONE

PREPARATION FOR THE ANOINTING

*A*nd when the man that had the line in his hand went forth eastward, he measured a thousand cubits, and he brought me through the waters; the waters were TO THE ANKLES. Again he measured a thousand, and brought me through the waters; the waters were TO THE KNEES. Again he measured a thousand, and brought me through; the waters were TO THE LOINS. Afterward he measured a thousand; and it was a river that I could not pass over: for the waters were risen, waters to swim in, a river that could not be passed over.

Ezekiel 47:3-4

Just as a river takes time to carve out the channel in which its waters flow, God's preparation in our lives, a preparation which enables us to be used as a blessing to others, does not happen overnight. It takes time, and it comes in stages.

Ezekiel saw water rising in three stages. First it came up to the ankles; then it came up to the knees; and, finally, it came up to the loins. This progression speaks to us about the process of growth that takes place in those who have chosen to be used of God in His Kingdom.

I see a likeness in these stages of spiritual growth to the corresponding stages of physical and emotional maturity that we experience as we grow up: first infancy or "babyhood," then childhood and, finally, maturity or "manhood."

Jesus revealed this same process of three stages of maturity in the parable of the vine and the branches. He said:

I am the true vine, and my Father is the husbandman. Every branch in me that beareth not fruit he taketh away: and every branch that beareth fruit, he purgeth it, that it may bring forth more fruit. Now ye are clean through the word which I have spoken unto you. Abide in me, and I in you. As the branch cannot bear fruit of itself, except it abide in the vine; no more can ye, except ye abide in me.

I am the vine, ye are the branches: He that abideth in me, and I in him, the same bringeth forth much fruit: for without me ye can do nothing. If a man abide not in me, he is cast forth as a branch, and is withered; and men gather them, and cast them into the fire, and they are burned. If ye abide in me, and my words abide in you, ye shall ask what ye will, and it shall be done unto you. Herein is my Father glorified, that ye bear much fruit; so shall ye be my disciples. John 15:1-8

It is important to note that we should bear fruit from the very beginning of our Christian experience, and any branch that does not bear fruit is in danger of being eliminated: *"Every branch in me that beareth not fruit he taketh away."* So every level of the Christian life is a level of fruitfulness, even the very first level, which corresponds to the infancy stage of our natural growth. We are born into the Kingdom to produce fruit for the Father's glory.

But we are not meant to continue forever on the first level of productivity. God has greater things in store for us. Just as we would all be disappointed, and even alarmed, if our babies didn't grow, God's plan for our lives will be thwarted if we do not steadily grow into the stature He has envisioned for us.

And, precisely because He has greater fruitfulness in mind for us, God must begin in each of us a process of purging or pruning: *"every branch that beareth fruit, he purgeth it, that it may bring forth more fruit."* This process of pruning does not represent a punishment, as some imagine. God isn't angry with us when we experience His purging. He is not trying to rob us of our joy. To the contrary: God is trying to prepare us for the greater things that are in store for us.

God cannot be satisfied that we simply bear some *"fruit."* He wants us to go on to greater fruitfulness, to bearing *"more fruit."* It is with this holy desire in mind that He applies His loving discipline to our lives. Every branch must be pruned, and the intended purpose is that it bear even *"more fruit."* Don't resist this process. It is for your benefit. It will make you a better man or woman in God. It will cause you to be more productive and lead you to the second stage of opportunity for faithfulness in the Lord.

But God is not even satisfied when we bear *"more fruit,"* and we must not be satisfied either. He cannot be satisfied, for He knows our true potential. He has destined us to bear *"much fruit,"* and nothing less can be satisfactory. We are to move from the initial stages of bearing *"fruit"* to bearing *"more fruit,"* to bearing *"much fruit."* This is God's will for every believer, and it should become our goal, as well.

Such a goal can only be accomplished as we learn to allow the anointing of God's Spirit to move in us and through us, to deepen and widen the channels and to constantly increase its movement, until it becomes a raging torrent within, a river of life, flowing out to all.

Two important things are said of this process that should motivate every single one of us to believe for it and to flow with it:

(1) *"Herein is my Father glorified."* Since every believer delights to glorify the Father, we cannot rest until our lives bear *"much fruit"* that abounds to His glory.

(2) *"So shall ye be my disciples."* When people are unconcerned about pleasing God and about bearing fruit for Him, it reveals that they are even in danger of losing their very souls, of not being counted as one of His.

Fruitfulness is the will of God for your life. Get with the program. Stop resisting God when He tries to cut a channel through your rock. Stop resisting His efforts to deepen and widen the flow of His presence in you. He knows what He is doing. Trust Him and stop struggling against His efforts. All that He is doing is for your benefit. He has your best interests at heart.

It is impossible for you to reach your true potential on your own. It is impossible for you to bear *"much fruit"* without the flow of God's life-giving rivers in your spirit. And it is impossible for those rivers to flow in the way He desires if He cannot first do the work of carving out the necessary channels in your life. Therefore, receive God's discipline with joy. Let Him work in your life. Let Him prune you and purge you through His Word.

David was one of those who recognized the ability of the Word to purge us. He said:

> *Wherewithal shall a young man cleanse his way,*
> *by taking heed thereto according to thy Word.*
>
> Psalm 119:9

Fully submit yourself to this cleansing process, knowing that the end of that process is fruitfulness. The principle of growth in stages is also illustrated in Jesus' teaching of the Parable of the Sower:

> *And he said, So is the kingdom of God, as if a man should cast seed into the ground; And should sleep, and rise night and day, and the seed should spring and grow up, he knoweth not how. For the earth bringeth forth fruit of herself; first the blade, then the ear, after that the full corn in the ear.*
>
> Mark 4:26-28

The first stage of growth is represented by His words, *"first the blade"*; the second stage is represented by the words *"then the ear"*; and the third and final stage is represented by the words *"after that the full corn in the ear."* This biblical principle is illustrated repeatedly throughout Scripture.

In Ezekiel's vision, the water he saw represents the river of living water, the anointing of God's Spirit on our lives, and he saw it increasing, getting deeper and wider. This is clearly God's will for each of us.

The important thing we must conclude from all of this is that the flowing of the rivers of God is so important to our spiritual welfare and the development of our true potential that we must consistently seek that flow, practicing those things which encourage and facilitate it, and avoiding those things which hinder or stop it.

If water is dammed up somewhere along a river, something happens. Because the natural flow of the water has been hindered, that river ceases to widen and deepen its channel. Therefore, it cannot grow any deeper and wider than it already is.

One of the most important things we can do, as those who desire God's best for our lives, is to recognize things that dam up or block the spiritual flow and cause the anointing to stagnate or dry up in our lives. If the Spirit of God does not have free reign in our lives, if He cannot flow through us consistently and regularly, our spiritual growth and potential are greatly diminished and even threatened altogether.

Speaking of natural dams: only recently scientists have begun to understand the way these man-made structures permanently change the landscape. They were built for their short-term benefits to society: for flood control, and to provide water and generate electric power for burgeoning populations. But the long-term damage dams do to their surroundings was not always understood. These days, as it is being discovered that the damage done by such a construction sometimes outweighs the good it can do, dams that were built many years ago are actually being blown up and removed so that rivers can resume their natural flow.

There is an important spiritual lesson in this: nothing can be permitted that creates a hindrance to the flow of the Spirit's anointing in us and through us. The long-term damage done is not worth whatever short-term advantage we might imagine.

Don't hesitate. Blow up every dam that blocks in any way the flow of the Holy Ghost in your life. Allowing even small ones to persist endangers your fruitfulness in God and even endangers the welfare of your soul. Blow them up!

The Scriptures point out clearly to us some of the things that can create spiritual dams in our lives and can hinder us in our quest for fruitfulness. We should learn to identify and eliminate these quickly, before they have a chance to form blockages that impede the flow of the rivers of living water in us.

Preparation For the Anointing

In his first letter to the Thessalonian believers, the Apostle Paul warned them of one such danger:

Quench not the Spirit.   1 Thessalonians 5:19

What does it mean to *"quench ... the Spirit"*? It means exactly what we are talking about. It means allowing anything at all to hinder the work the Holy Ghost is endeavoring to do in our lives.

Paul continued:

Despise not prophesyings, ... hold fast that which is good.   1 Thessalonians 5:20-21

Paul meant then that we should not resist the good things God's Spirit is doing in us, and that we should allow nothing that others do to hinder that move either.

Each of us must determine to cooperate with the Spirit, to yield ourselves to the working of the Holy Ghost and not quench Him by resisting His work in us.

This is a matter of faith. If we believe that God loves us and is doing what is best for us, how can we resist Him? How can we quench, purposely or otherwise, what He wants to do in us?

Have faith in God, and that faith will lead you to cooperate fully with His desires for your life. That faith will lead you to yield yourself to Him unreservedly. That faith will make you responsive to his promptings and open to His manifestations, whatever they might be, and wherever they might lead you.

This element of faith is confirmed by Paul in his teaching to the Romans:

> *Having then gifts differing according to the grace that is given to us, whether prophecy, let us prophesy according to the proportion of faith.*
>
> Romans 12:6

It takes faith to cooperate with the Holy Spirit, to trust that God knows what He is doing, and that everything He does in us and through us will be for our ultimate benefit.

It helps when we are able to recognize the moving of the Holy Ghost and to have some understanding of His gifts. Then it is easier to cooperate with Him, by faith, as He seeks to manifest Himself in our lives. And when we have this understanding, we can do the opposite of quenching the Holy Ghost, which is to encourage the Holy Ghost to work in us.

In the late 70s, while I was still in Bible college in Dayton, Ohio, I was fasting and praying and asking God to use me in the gifts of the Spirit. I had a part-time job in a gas station to help me make ends meet, and one day a gentleman came by in a delivery van asking for directions. As we stood there together looking at the map of the city, I experienced a sudden sense that this man was sick and an urge to pray for him.

I found it rather strange to have these feelings in a service station lot and with a man I had never met and knew nothing about. I glanced over at him to see if he looked sick, but he looked okay to me.

I was wondering what to do next when a customer pulled up at the pumps, and had to excuse myself to attend to him. When I had finished serving that customer and turned back to help the delivery man, I found that he was leaving. He had apparently found the location he was looking for on the map and no longer needed my help.

I experienced a sinking feeling as I watched the man drive away. God had been trying to answer my prayer, and I had been too slow to respond.

What had made me feel that the man was sick and needed prayer? There was nothing visibly wrong with him, and he said nothing to give me that idea. I came to the conclusion that sensing his need must have been a word of knowledge from the Spirit of God.

If I had responded, instead of questioning what I felt and delaying action until it was too late, no doubt God would have manifested His healing power in that place, and the man would have gone away with a miracle. I felt that I had quenched the

Spirit and made a determination that I would never do it again.

The lesson I learned that day in a filling station in Dayton, Ohio, caused me to make a covenant with God that I would never again quench His Spirit. I vowed that I would cooperate with Him fully, whether I understood what He was doing or not. And since that time God has been faithful to allow me many more similar opportunities to flow in the gifts of the Spirit, to pray for people in need, and to see the results of His grace at work. These experiences have consistently deepened the flow of the river of God in my life.

God is so good! He was not angry with me for not cooperating with Him. He was disappointed because, after all, He was only trying to enrich my spiritual life and experience. He was so merciful and longsuffering to me as I learned His ways, coming to me again and again, and giving me opportunities to learn from my mistakes and to step into new and rewarding experiences.

Quench not the Spirit! What a wonderful lesson!

When we hinder the work of the Spirit of God in our lives, He is grieved, much as a loving earthly father is grieved when a son spurns his love. If we love God, we will learn to avoid anything that grieves His Spirit. Paul wrote:

> *Let no corrupt communication proceed out of your mouth, but that which is good to the use of edify-*

Preparation For the Anointing

ing, that it may minister grace unto the hearers. And grieve not the Holy Spirit of God, whereby ye are sealed unto the day of redemption.

Ephesians 4:29-30

Some people have difficulty understanding the concept of grieving God. They don't understand that God seeks our fellowship, just as we seek His. They don't realize that God created us for His fellowship and that He is saddened when, for any reason, we choose not to be with Him or we choose to ignore His will for us. We can bring God joy, and we can bring Him sorrow.

You can grieve God's Spirit, and grieving the Holy Ghost will definitely hinder the flow of His anointing in your life. It can hinder or destroy entirely the work of deepening and widening that you need in order to become a fruitful believer. If you grieve the Spirit, you cannot go on to higher levels of anointing — until whatever is causing God sadness is removed. You even put your very soul at risk when God is not happy with you.

There are many ways that we can grieve the heart of God. The one mentioned in this passage concerns our speech. We are to guard our tongues that *"no corrupt communication proceed out of our mouth[s]."* Instead, we are to speak *"that which is good to the use of edifying."* What we say should *"minister grace unto the hearers."*

So, one of the ways we often grieve God is by hurting one another with our words. If they are *"corrupt,"* influenced by the world around us, if they are not *"good,"* if they do nothing toward the *"edifying"* of others, and if they clearly do not *"minister grace unto the hearers,"* our words grieve the heart of God.

God wants to inspire in us words that are not corrupted by this world, words that speak of good things, words that edify those around us and words that minister God's love and mercy to those that hear them. The Spirit's words are described in this way:

> *But he that prophesieth speaketh unto men to edification, and exhortation, and comfort.*
>
> 1 Corinthians 14:3

The ministry of the Spirit of God is to build people up, not to tear them down, and if you and I are to be used of God to bless the world around us, we must develop a conversation that is edifying, that builds people up; and we must learn to avoid destructive conversation, that which tears people down.

If we are to move into the greater degrees of anointing that God has reserved for us, we must learn the language of the Spirit. He always speaks *"grace to the hearers,"* and so must we.

Preparation For the Anointing

Paul continued, showing us more of what grieves the heart of God:

> *Let all bitterness, and wrath, and anger, and clamor, and evil speaking, be put away from you, with all malice.*   Ephesians 4:31

This word *bitterness* comes from a root word that means *to bite*. Bitterness is a spirit that I call "the dog spirit," and many Christians have it. As soon as a certain person's name is mentioned, they begin to bite that person with their unkind words. Speaking evil of others seems to be the favorite pastime of many these days. The spirit of bitterness is alive and well.

But we must *"put away all malice."* This passage was written to Christians, not to unbelievers. So believers are guilty of harboring malice in their hearts and must *"put [it] away,"* get rid of it.

From this word *malice* we get the word *malignant,* meaning *likely to cause death,* and that's exactly what malice produces. Christians actually cause the spiritual death of other Christians because of their *"bitterness, and wrath, and anger, and clamor, and evil speaking."* If your conduct is discouraging another member of God's family, you are in trouble with the Father. He is grieved by your actions.

Paul advised:

And be ye kind one to another, tenderhearted,
forgiving one another, even as God for Christ's
sake hath forgiven you.   Ephesians 4:32

People are not generally, *"kind," "tenderhearted,"* and *"forgiving"*; but God is. And if we expect to house the Spirit of God and to experience all the benefits of His presence with us and in us, we must learn to be *"kind," "tenderhearted," and "forgiving,"* as well. If not, we cannot please our heavenly Father.

Learn what pleases God and what displeases Him. Learn what brings Him joy and what grieves Him. Then, start doing what pleases Him and avoiding what grieves Him.

Jesus was anointed of God and went about doing good everywhere, blessing everyone He met. It was because He understood the heart of the Father and strove to please Him in all things.

If you desire to have an intimate relationship with the Holy Ghost, you cannot be constantly causing Him sorrow. If someone did that to you, sooner or later you would start doing what was necessary to avoid that person, as much as possible. And if we continually grieve the Holy Ghost and cause Him sorrow, He ceases to manifest Himself in us. If our uncaring actions continue, He is forced to withdraw from us as well, and our fellowship with God is endangered.

Preparation For the Anointing

Once, when I was teaching a Bible school class on "The Authority of the Believer," I was reminding the class that Jesus had great authority over evil spirits and was able to cast them out. If we expected to take authority over demons and cast them out, as He did, I told them, we must walk closely with the Spirit of God, as He did.

As I was emphasizing the need to become more like Jesus, I suddenly saw the Lord standing near me. From the look in His eyes, I could sense that He wanted to come closer, but He approached with great caution, as though He had been wounded before. When I saw this expression in the Lord's eyes, my spirit was broken within me, and I realized as never before how important it is for us to be kind and tender to one another. For we hurt Him when we hurt one another, and this forces Him to keep His distance from us. *Grieve not the Holy Spirit of God!*

Quenching the Spirit is an act that places a dam in the way of the flow of the Spirit of God in your life. Grieving the Spirit of God blocks the flow of His anointing and hinders or even stops the process of cutting out rivers that is so important to your fruitfulness in the Kingdom of God. *Quench not! Grieve not!*

Some people actually come to despise the Spirit and His work:

*Of how much sorer punishment, suppose ye, shall
he be thought worthy, who hath trodden under
foot the Son of God, and hath counted the blood
of the covenant, wherewith he was sanctified, an
unholy thing, and hath done despite unto the
Spirit of grace?*   Hebrews 10:29

It is altogether possible to turn against the work-
ings of God's Spirit and become an opposer of all
that He desires to do. The writer of Hebrews gives
us this example.

The NIV translates this phrase *"hath done despite"*
as *"has insulted."* Can you imagine men standing
up to God and actually insulting Him? The thought
makes me shiver, but it happens.

The men in question were insulting the Holy
Ghost by denying who Christ really was. God declared Jesus to be His holy Son, to have pure and
sinless blood in His veins. This uniquely qualified
Him to be the sacrifice for our sins. Those who deny
that fact are insulting the Spirit of God, for He came
to glorify Jesus.

Despising God's Spirit, insulting Him, is a dangerous game that men should not play. When God
departs from our lives, what do we have left?

Quenching the Spirit, grieving the Spirit, despising the Spirit: let all these dams be blown up and
removed by the dynamite of the Word of God:

Preparation For the Anointing

Now ye are clean through the word which I have spoken unto you. John 15:3

Sanctify them through thy truth: thy word is truth. John 17:17

As you and I receive the Word of God into our lives and act upon it continuously, every dam, every impediment to the Spirit's flow, will be removed and the Holy Spirit will have free access to flow through us, widening and deepening the river bed, and taking us from one degree of glory to another and from one degree of fruitfulness to another. This is God's will for your life.

CHAPTER TWO

THE PROPHETIC ANOINTING

A nd when the man that had the line in his hand went forth eastward, he measured a thousand cubits, and he brought me through the waters; the waters were TO THE ANKLES.
                                                    Ezekiel 47:3

There were three anointings in which Jesus operated during His incarnation here on Earth. He was prophet, priest and king. Today, nearly two thousand years after the return of our Lord to Heaven, all three of these anointings — the prophetic anointing, the priestly anointing, and the kingly anointing — are available to the Body of Christ and to the individual believer.

The first anointing that we receive, as Spirit-filled believers, is the prophetic anointing. The Scriptures declare: *"they shall prophesy."*

31

And it shall come to pass in the last days, saith God, I will pour out of my Spirit upon all flesh: and your sons and your daughters shall prophesy, and your young men shall see visions, and your old men shall dream dreams: And on my servants and on my handmaidens I will pour out in those days of my Spirit; and they shall prophesy.
Acts 2:17-18

When we are filled with the Holy Ghost, just as one hundred and twenty believers were on the Day of Pentecost, we move into a prophetic anointing and begin to operate in the three gifts of the Spirit which fall under the category we commonly call "vocal gifts." All the gifts of the Spirit are listed in Paul's first letter to the Corinthians:

But the manifestation of the Spirit is given to every man to profit withal. For to one is given by the Spirit the word of wisdom; to another the word of knowledge by the same Spirit; To another faith by the same Spirit; to another the gifts of healing by the same Spirit; To another the working of miracles; to another PROPHECY; to another discerning OF SPIRITS; TO ANOTHER divers kinds of tongues; to another THE INTERPRETATION OF TONGUES: But all these worketh that one and the selfsame Spirit, dividing to every man severally as he will.
1 Corinthians 12:7-11

The Prophetic Anointing

We can roughly divide these nine gifts of the Spirit into three groups of three each. The first of these groups, the vocal gifts, or gifts of utterance (as some refer to them), are speaking with tongues, interpretation of tongues and the gift of prophecy. I believe that these three gifts all come under the heading "the prophetic anointing."

The prophetic anointing enables us to speak. It gives us voice and enables us to communicate God's wonders to others. It is *"the blade"* referred to in Mark 4, the *"waters to the ankles"* of Ezekiel 47, the *"fruit"* of John 15, the first degree of anointing in our spiritual lives. It is the place we all begin when we are newly saved and filled with the Holy Ghost.

I don't know of a single believer who began his spiritual life in the priestly anointing or in the kingly anointing. I have known many, however, who were newly saved and filled, who immediately entered into a prophetic anointing, and I am convinced that this is the scriptural pattern for believers today.

We can see this pattern in Acts 2 with the original outpouring of the Spirit on the Day of Pentecost:

> *And when the day of Pentecost was fully come, they were all with one accord in one place. And suddenly there came a sound from heaven as of a rushing mighty wind, and it filled all the house where they were sitting. And there appeared unto*

*them cloven tongues like as of fire, and it sat
upon each of them. And they were all filled with
the Holy Ghost, and began to speak with other
tongues, as the Spirit gave them utterance.*

Acts 2:1-4

The same pattern appears again in Acts 10, when
Peter preached to the Gentiles in Caesarea and the
Spirit was poured out upon them:

*While Peter yet spake these words, the Holy Ghost
fell on all them which heard the word. And they
of the circumcision which believed were aston-
ished, as many as came with Peter, because that
on the Gentiles also was poured out the gift of
the Holy Ghost. For they heard them speak with
tongues, and magnify God.*   Acts 10:44-46

The pattern was repeated yet again, in Acts 19,
when Paul prayed for some disciples of John the
Baptist in Ephesus:

*And when Paul had laid his hands upon them,
the Holy Ghost came on them; and they spake
with tongues, and prophesied.*   Acts 19:6

From these and other scriptures, it seems appar-
ent that the prophetic anointing is the first anointing that all new Spirit-filled believers experience.

The Prophetic Anointing

The first flow of the Holy Ghost in our lives makes us very vocal for the Lord. That vocal gift manifests itself in the ability to communicate to others what God has done for us. This begins a prophetic flow that will strengthen and grow as we yield to it.

God spoke to John the Revelator:

The testimony of Jesus Christ is the Spirit of prophecy. Revelation 19:10

When we begin to testify about the Lord Jesus Christ, even though we may simply be giving our story of salvation, a prophetic anointing is unleashed in our lives. If this prophetic anointing is encouraged and exercised, it will grow into an ability to speak for Christ and to preach the Gospel with power.

The gift of prophecy is a further manifestation of the prophetic anointing. Prophecy can be defined as *speaking in a known language by inspiration of the Holy Ghost.* This is a spontaneous manifestation of the Holy Ghost and is totally unpremeditated. It does not involve sharing from memory, but rather receiving fresh thoughts from Heaven as we speak, guided by the Spirit of God. When prophesying, we say things we had not anticipated saying, because we speak by inspiration of the Holy Ghost. He breathes into us that which He wants us to speak.

It was through the manifestation of the prophetic anointing that the Bible was given to us. Speaking of this gift, the Bible declares:

> *We have also a more sure word of prophecy;*
> *whereunto ye do well that ye take heed, as unto a*
> *light that shineth in a dark place, until the day*
> *dawn, and the day star arise in your hearts:*
> *Knowing this first, that no prophecy of the scrip-*
> *ture is of any private interpretation. For the*
> *prophecy came not in old time by the will of man:*
> *but holy men of God spake as they were moved*
> *by the Holy Ghost.* 2 Peter 1:19-21

The Spirit of God moves us to speak to others about our Lord and His Word.

When Peter was first filled with the Spirit, on the Day of Pentecost, he immediately stood up and began to speak to the crowd that had gathered to watch what was happening there on Mount Zion. There was something new and unusual about Peter's speech that day. He began by sharing a scripture from the book of Joel, but then he declared to the witnesses that what they were seeing that day was a fulfillment of Joel's promise:

> *But Peter, standing up with the eleven, lifted up*
> *his voice, and said unto them, Ye men of Judaea,*
> *and all ye that dwell at Jerusalem, be this known*

unto you, and hearken to my words: For these
are not drunken, as ye suppose, seeing it is but
the third hour of the day. But this is that which
was spoken by the prophet Joel.   Acts 2:14-16

Peter may have had some knowledge of what he
was sharing from Joel, but the fact that it was being fulfilled that very day was a revelation from
the Holy Ghost. Peter might not have related this
strange experience to the prophecy of Joel, if he
had not been under a prophetic anointing.

What Peter spoke that day explained to the
people the strange manifestations they were wit-
nessing. It was not easy for them to understand how
the disciples could be acting like drunken men when
they hadn't had anything intoxicating to drink that
morning, but God's Word made it clear. *"This is
that ... ."*

The experience on the Day of Pentecost was
Peter's initial experience in the prophetic realm,
but he would have many more similar experiences
in the years to come.

The anointing that was upon Peter that day made
a great impact upon the people who heard him
speak:

Now when they heard this, they were pricked in
their heart, and said unto Peter and to the rest of

*the apostles, Men and brethren, what shall we
do?*   Acts 2:37

When we are being moved by the Holy Ghost to
speak from the Word of God, or from our personal
testimony and experience, men's hearts are touched
by the truth of what we speak, and they are moved
to respond to Christ. This is the power of the prophetic anointing which God has placed upon our
lives.

When we are faithful to give our testimonies and
to speak the Word of God, the prophetic anointing
that is upon us will increase, and we may even be
used to give a message to the whole body of believers. What a privilege that is!

What we say to the Body of Christ should always
be something that edifies, exhorts and comforts:

> *But he that prophesieth speaketh unto men to
> edification, and exhortation, and comfort.*
>   1 Corinthians 14:3

Some have a mistaken concept of prophecy: that
it is always revealing either someone's future or
something from someone's past. Prophecy may deal
with the past, present or future, but is not necessarily a revelation of something that is hidden or
unknown. Prophecy may be simply a word of encouragement (*"edification"*), a word of *"exhortation,"*

or a word of *"comfort."* I like to say, "The gift of prophecy builds up, stirs up, and cheers up the hearers." I have found that to be the case.

If we always function under the anointing of the Spirit of God, people will be stirred and blessed and encouraged when we speak; for God knows just how to reach their hearts. In the process, we are blessed; for as the Spirit flows through us, God is carving out rivers among the rocks of our souls. The result will be much greater blessing, both for us and for those to whom we minister.

Be faithful to your prophetic calling, and God will enlarge it. In the Parable of the Talents, Jesus showed that those who don't properly use the talents and abilities He has given will lose them and that those who are faithful and use their talents will receive even more:

Then he which had received the one talent came and said, Lord, I knew thee that thou art an hard man, reaping where thou hast not sown, and gathering where thou hast not strawed: And I was afraid, and went and hid thy talent in the earth: lo, there thou hast that is thine. His lord answered and said unto him, Thou wicked and slothful servant, thou knewest that I reap where I sowed not, and gather where I have not strawed: Thou oughtest therefore to have put my money to the exchangers, and then at my coming I should have

received mine own with usury. Take therefore the
talent from him, and give it unto him which hath
ten talents.   Matthew 25:24-28

We must be faithful with what we have been
given by God. We must allow our gifts to operate
and to bless those who need a touch from God. In
doing so, our lives are also enriched and enlarged.

Many believers today don't really know the
power they have or how to put it to work. Personally, I believe that the most important thing we can
do is to associate with prophetic people. In other
words, we need to be with people who are obedient to God in this respect and in an atmosphere
where obeying God prophetically is not only permitted but encouraged.

When young Saul, who was destined to become
Israel's first king, came in contact with some people
who were moving in the prophetic realm, he too
began to prophesy. I believe that this is an important biblical principal. We need to associate ourselves with people of anointing in order to be
anointed ourselves:

Then Samuel took a vial of oil, and poured it upon
his [Saul's] head, and kissed him, and said, Is it
not because the LORD hath anointed thee to be
captain over his inheritance? When thou art de-
parted from me to day, then thou shalt find two

men by Rachel's sepulchre in the border of Benjamin at Zelzah; and they will say unto thee, The asses which thou wentest to seek are found: and, lo, thy father hath left the care of the asses, and sorroweth for you, saying, What shall I do for my son?

Then shalt thou go on forward from thence, and thou shalt come to the plain of Tabor, and there shall meet thee three men going up to God to Bethel, one carrying three kids, and another carrying three loaves of bread, and another carrying a bottle of wine: And they will salute thee, and give thee two loaves of bread; which thou shalt receive of their hands.

After that thou shalt come to the hill of God, where is the garrison of the Philistines: and it shall come to pass, when thou art come thither to the city, that thou shalt meet a company of prophets coming down from the high place with a psaltery, and a tabret, and a pipe, and a harp, before them; and they shall prophesy: And the Spirit of the LORD will come upon thee, and thou shalt prophesy with them, and shalt be turned into another man. And let it be, when these signs are come unto thee, that thou do as occasion serve thee; for God is with thee.   1 Samuel 10:1-7

Because God wanted Saul to partake of the prophetic mantle, He sent him to a place where he could be with anointed prophets, a place of association and opportunity. I believe, therefore, that the best way for a person who wants to be used in the prophetic realm to get started is to associate themselves with those who are functioning in that anointing and who are open to the development of the gifts of others.

Another such case in Scripture, also involved Saul:

> *So David fled, and escaped, and came to Samuel to Ramah, and told him all that Saul had done to him. And he and Samuel went and dwelt in Naioth. And it was told Saul, saying, Behold, David is at Naioth in Ramah. And Saul sent messengers to take David: and when they saw the company of the prophets prophesying, and Samuel standing as appointed over them, the Spirit of God was upon the messengers of Saul, and they also prophesied. And when it was told Saul, he sent other messengers, and they prophesied likewise. And Saul sent messengers again the third time, and they prophesied also.*
>
> 1 Samuel 19:18-21

When you get around people with a prophetic anointing, it is much easier to enter into your prophetic calling and begin to prophesy like the others. It will happen if you go up to *"the hill of God"*

and find *"a company of prophets,"* people who are
flowing in the anointing and allowing others to flow
in it, as well.

Some would challenge my assertion that God
wants all of His children to have a prophetic anointing, but Moses also thought they should. When
some of the elders who assisted him in leading the
people of Israel through the wilderness felt a touch
of his anointing and began to prophesy, some questioned it. They wondered if it was right for others
to prophesy like Moses did. Even Joshua was not
sure if it was right. Wouldn't this weaken Moses'
ability to lead the people? Moses answered the crit-
ics:

> *Enviest thou for my sake? Would God that all
> the LORD'S people were prophets, and that the
> LORD would put His Spirit upon them!*
> Numbers 11:29

Would Moses have said such a thing of his own
accord? Or was it a revelation from God? There can
be no doubt that God wants His people to function
prophetically, to flow in prophetic anointing
through the gift of tongues, interpretation of
tongues, prophecy and through the testimony of
the Lord Jesus in their lives.

It is necessary for us to differentiate between the
gift of prophecy and the ministry of a prophet.

There is a great difference. Every believer is called to the prophetic anointing, but not every believer is called to the office of the prophet.

In writing to the Corinthians, Paul asked rhetorically:

Are all prophets?   1 Corinthians 12:29

The understood answer was no. Just as not every believer is an apostle, and not every believer is a teacher, and not every believer is a worker of miracles, not everyone can be expected to assume the office of the prophet. That does not, however, preclude every believer from having a prophetic anointing.

So what is the difference? I believe the primary difference is that the prophet is gifted with special revelation. Isaiah, Jeremiah, Ezekiel and Daniel were prophets in the fullest sense. They didn't just prophesy. They held a special place in society and were looked up to as men of revelation who could lead the country forward.

The anointing for the prophetic office includes the gift of the word of wisdom, the gift of the word of knowledge and, generally speaking, the discerning of spirits. So the prophet not only has the gift of prophecy, or the prophetic anointing, but he also has the revelatory gifts operative in his life. They are part of his everyday equipment.

The Prophetic Anointing

The Scriptures confirm this concept:

Surely the Lord GOD will do nothing, but he revealeth his secret unto his servants the prophets.   Amos 3:3

Not every believer is cognizant of what God is doing, but prophets are. Not every believer can warn a nation of impending judgment, but prophets can. Just as a teacher can be expected to teach, and an evangelist can be expected to evangelize, a prophet can be expected to have prophetic revelation. It is part of his ministry.

Not everyone is a prophet. Not everyone has a special ministry of revelation. Not everyone is called to give divine guidance to the Body of Believers. Yet every believer can prophesy and speak forth words of edification, exhortation and comfort to those in need.

The office of the prophet is one of the official functions of ministry outlined in the Word of God. Although we are all called to be mature, for example, God chooses certain *"elders,"* those who demonstrate greater maturity, and give them a special office in the Church. They are charged with the care of His little ones and His outreach to the world around us.

If someone has an official function, in a secular sense, such as a law enforcement officer, we expect him to perform certain duties related to that function. A law enforcement officer keeps the peace and makes arrests when that peace is broken. He has a job description and recognized responsibilities. The same is true in the Church.

The Bible puts forth five basic ministries or offices that must function if the Church is to grow and prosper:

> *And he gave some, APOSTLES; and some, PROPHETS; and some, EVANGELISTS; and some, PASTORS and TEACHERS; For the perfecting of the saints, for the work of the ministry, for the edifying of the body of Christ: Till we all come in the unity of the faith, and of the knowledge of the Son of God, unto a perfect man, unto the measure of the stature of the fulness of Christ: That we henceforth be no more children, tossed to and fro, and carried about with every wind of doctrine, by the sleight of men, and cunning craftiness, whereby they lie in wait to deceive;*
> Ephesians 4:11-14

These are official functions or offices of the Church that have attached to them specific duties and responsibilities. They each have a certain job description, and we expect those who assume these offices to perform their assigned duties. Prophets are expected to hear from God and to consistently have divine guidance for the Church and for the nation.

Not everyone can expect to minister revelation. This demands maturity and seriousness. Those who prophesy do not necessarily have the gift of the word of knowledge and word of wisdom. If you are called simply to give words of edification, exhortation, and comfort, don't try to step outside that calling and to minister in a function that does not pertain to you.

This is the reason that the Apostles of the early Church always placed "elders" in charge of ministry. It was these seasoned and wise men who administered the laying on of hands and the revelatory prophecy to the whole Body.

Paul wrote to his spiritual son Timothy:

> *Neglect not the gift that is in thee, which was given thee by prophecy, with the laying on of the hands of the presbytery.* 1 Timothy 4:14

The *"presbytery"* was composed of the *"elders"* and functionaries of the Church, the recognized leaders of the local body. These were the men who were charged with prophetic direction. These were men gifted with the word of knowledge and the word of wisdom and a deep sense of God's continued revelation in their lives. They were not novices — in any sense of the word!

We all have to start somewhere, but although any believer may be used in a prophetic sense, we need sincere, proven and appointed people in serious offices of leadership within the Church.

As our earthly children grow and develop, we want them to take on new responsibilities and develop new talents, but that doesn't make them the head of the house. Headship requires maturity and a proven track record. Therefore, we must be careful not to overstep our bounds.

As we grow, we gain insights and ability, but until God puts His finger on us for official service, we must respect His order within the family. Having insight and ability does not give us license to function in a position to which God has not called us and in which others have not confirmed us. This is a truth that needs to be emphasized more in the Body today.

The Old Testament leaders operated schools for the prophets, centers where the young ones who felt a call of God to excellence in the prophetic ministry could sit at the feet of the elders and learn. It is easy to see from various Old Testament passages that "the sons of the prophets" had a great respect for those who were already recognized prophets and did not try to take their place.

Learn to operate within the bounds God has set for each of us in His Word. Every river has a river bed, and if it gets out of its banks, we consider it to be out of control and dangerous. As long as it stays within its determined course, it serves a useful purpose, but as soon as it breaks forth over its natural boundaries, it begins to do great damage to things around it.

A river that is out of control will destroy lives and property, but a river that is channeled and harnessed, operating within official boundaries, will result in the blessing of many people's lives. Please understand this. It is for your good, as well as the good of the many others you can bless.

The prophetic ministry, therefore, requires great discipline, great self-control; and those who train potential prophets look for this quality in those who seek to be students of the prophetic realm. Can a person be given opportunity without them abusing it and taking advantage of that opportunity? If you give them time in a service, do they use it wisely? If you let them speak, is what they say anointed? Does it bless people? Some get totally out of control, taking up valuable time for things that profit no one, and then they blame their lack of discipline on the Spirit of God, saying that they "just couldn't help themselves."

One of the tests of discipleship that young prophets need to pass is that of being able to control themselves under the anointing of God and to do only what they are asked to do by a mature and responsible leader. This is a serious part of the process of carving out rivers among the rocks. God has said:

> *Let all things be done decently and in order.*
> 1 Corinthians 14:40

If we are obedient to those who are over us in the Lord, and if we consistently operate within the boundaries and the guidelines that we are given, we will find the rivers widening and deepening in our lives, and we will be recognized not only for our giftedness, but for our ability to function in the prescribed order in the House of God. And only when we learn to flow in the prophetic anointing within the boundaries of the principles God has set forth for us will we be able to move on to other levels of anointing.

Some who have a very great calling in God never fulfill their potential because they get in with the wrong crowd. They prefer to fellowship with those who have no rules, no guidelines. Anything goes. Everything is accepted. But the Bible advises:

> *He that walketh with wise men shall be wise: but*
> *a companion of fools shall be destroyed.*
> Proverbs 13:20

I would encourage everyone who is beginning to flow in prophetic anointing to seek out wise men and women of God, men and women who have learned to operate within boundaries and guidelines. We are to worship God both *"in spirit and in truth"* (John 4:23), that is we are to have a balance of the spontaneous flow of the Holy Ghost and the unchanging guidance of the Word of God.

The last great move of the Spirit that we experienced in our country and around the world eventually fizzled because it was a movement of flow without form. There were many good aspects of the revival. People went forth everywhere, preaching, prophesying, casting out devils, and laying hands on the sick; but the results of their efforts were often temporary because they scattered like the wind without any real guidance about what they were to do and how they were to do it.

Now, God is restoring order to the Church. He is restoring the ministry of apostles and other mature leaders so that this coming wave of glory will bear eternal fruit for the Kingdom. It will have structure and order brought about by godly church government. This present-day move of God, which will reach its climax with the coming of Christ, will have not only a great flow of the Spirit, but will also have biblical order. Rivers will stay within their banks and remain a blessing, rather than wander off to do possible damage.

Jesus is coming back, and His Church will receive Him with *"great glory."* It will be molded and disciplined into a *"glorious church, having neither spot nor wrinkle."*

Seek out your *"hill of God"*; find your *"prophetic company"*; and let the anointing which is upon them come also upon you. Then, learn from these wise men and women. Maintain a spirit of meekness and lowliness. Be teachable and open to correction. If you are willing to do these things, the Spirit of God will have free reign in your life.

Many people never get this far because they refuse to be teachable, and even more fail because they absolutely refuse to accept correction. But this is an important part of our spiritual development. Anyone who is not willing to receive, not only instruction but reproof and correction, is not fit to function in a position of spiritual responsibility.

God is looking for faithful vessels in these last days, men and women who have willingly submitted themselves to the necessary shaping and forming and molding and polishing, that they may bring honor and glory to the Lord Jesus Christ and His work, and not bring reproach, as some have done in the past.

Why it is necessary for God to put students of prophecy under the tutelage of others who are seasoned and mature should be obvious. It was true even of Jesus' chosen disciples. An incident in the life of Peter makes the point:

When Judas had betrayed Jesus to the Roman soldiers and was leading them into the Garden of

The Prophetic Anointing

Gethsemane, where he knew the Master was praying, Peter saw the group of men approaching the Lord and did a very foolish thing. He pulled out a sword and swung at one of the men, cutting his ear off. Peter was an impulsive person, and this was just his gut reaction to a troubling situation that he didn't understand.

Jesus didn't praise Peter for what he had done. Threatening the life of another human being was not a spiritual act, and Jesus rebuked Peter for it.

To me, Peter was like so many other young, eager believers. He had a great vision; he was quick with the word (and the sword); and he was going to conquer the world, in his own way.

Surely Peter must have felt remorse for having injured the man, named in Scripture as Malcus, but it was too late. He could apologize, but he couldn't undo the damage he had inflicted. Thank God that Jesus healed the man. But the sad thing is that we have a lot of Peters going around wounding a lot of Malcuses.

If you jump out into ministry prematurely, as young people tend to do, you may end up hurting a lot of people in your zeal. Take heed to this warning. Some people have been so hurt that they don't ever want to hear about the Lord or the Gospel or the Church or preachers again, and someone will answer for that when we stand before God. Zeal must be tempered by wisdom and experience and understanding and, most of all, compassion.

When you go out for the Lord, you want to be a walking model of what you preach, and you want to understand and demonstrate the nature of Christ to others. Then the Lord won't have to go behind you healing everyone you hurt.

If you will be submissive to mature believers, they will help you to avoid making these mistakes and help you when you unintentionally do. Paul wrote to Timothy:

> *Take heed unto thyself, and unto the doctrine; continue in them: for in doing this thou shalt both save thyself, and them that hear thee.*
>
> 1 Timothy 4:16

What a powerful promise! By taking heed to do things in the proper and prescribed way, Timothy would *"save [himself]"* and he would save *"them that hear[d] [him]."*

Jesus is a perfect example of this concept. Although He knew the Father's will for His life very early, He waited until He was seasoned before He took on the great task at hand. He set a pattern for us to follow, as did those He personally trained. And if we are willing to follow His example, we have a great promise:

> *Verily, verily, I say unto you, He that believeth on me, the works that I do shall he do also; and*

The Prophetic Anointing

*greater works than these shall he do; because I go
unto my Father.*   John 14:12

The proof of the validity of this promise is that
those who followed Jesus continued to do those
same miracles, even after He had returned to
Heaven.

The prophetic anointing, *"first the blade," "waters
to the ankles," "fruit,"* is received by association with
those who are functioning in the prophetic realm,
and it is developed and becomes permanently fruitful through submission to order in the Body. Let
God do His desired work in you.

Many churches are *"hill[s] of God"* where God
has *"a company of prophets"* prepared and where He
is calling His Sauls to be anointed and to become
"another man." I am sure that many of those who
will read this book will do so precisely because they
have such a calling. If YOU are one of those, I urge
you today not to skip any of the steps necessary to
move toward fruitfulness in your personal life and
ministry. Don't be in a hurry. Give God time to cut
those rivers wide and deep. He has a great work
for you to do, but it can be done only when His
glory flows freely in and through your life.

God is searching for servants in these last days
through whom He can pour forth prophetic anointing in mighty demonstration, speaking forth the
Word of the Lord, and confirming it by signs and
wonders. He said He would pour out His Spirit

"upon all flesh," then went on to single out *"servants"* and *"handmaidens."* Although *"all flesh"* will receive the outpouring of the Holy Ghost, it is the *"servants"* and the *"handmaidens"* that God will use in a unique way. He said *"they shall prophesy."*

Let us become the servants and handmaidens of our God. Let us become men and women scrubbed of our own personal agenda and ready to do His bidding. Let us serve Him by serving others in the Body of Christ. Let us follow the example of Mary, His earthly mother:

> *And Mary said, Behold the handmaid of the Lord; be it unto me according to thy word. And the angel departed from her.*　　Luke 1:38

Say to God today, "I am ready to obey You in all things. Because I desire the fulfillment of my promised ministry, I am willing to submit myself to the process of preparation necessary to receive this ministry."

Now, attach yourself to *"a company"* where you can develop the depth of channel you need and start blowing up the dams that are keeping you from the flow of God's very best for your life. And don't stop; keep going deeper, moving from glory to glory. Let your anointing become a raging stream that will flow out to bless all those around you. This is the will of God for your life.

The waters are *"TO THE ANKLES."*

CHAPTER THREE

THE PRIESTLY ANOINTING

*A*gain *he measured a thousand, and brought me through the waters; the waters were TO THE KNEES.*

Ezekiel 47:4

The water is rising. God wants to do greater things in and through His people. A second anointing awaits us, the priestly anointing:

But ye are a chosen generation, a royal priesthood, an holy nation, a peculiar people; that ye should shew forth the praises of him who hath called you out of darkness into his marvelous light. 1 Peter 2:9

Our heavenly Father has destined us to become His priests on the Earth, and not a single believer is

57

excluded. We have been made *"kings and priests unto God"*:

> *And from Jesus Christ, who is the faithful witness, and the first begotten of the dead, and the prince of the kings of the earth. Unto him that loved us, and washed us from our sins in his own blood, And hath made us kings and priests unto God and his Father; to him be glory and dominion for ever and ever. Amen.* Revelation 1:5-6

From time immemorial God had a plan to establish a nation of priests. He took Abraham out of the corruption of Ur and sent him to a far land so that he could begin to form a new and holy nation. When the sons of Jacob left the precepts of Jehovah, the entire nation had to be forced into bondage in Egypt — to preserve it. Then, after four hundred years of slavery, God brought the Israelites out of Egypt with a strong arm, that they might form, again, the holy nation He desired.

Under the new covenant, the Church, made up of the redeemed, is God's *"holy nation"* and His *"royal priesthood."* Each of us, through the name of the Lord Jesus Christ, has the privilege of ministering unto the Lord, of bringing before Him our sacrifices of praise and worship. The writer of Hebrews declared:

The Priestly Anointing

*By Jesus therefore let us offer the sacrifice of praise
to God continually, that is, the fruit of our lips
giving thanks to His name.*   Hebrews 13:15

This holy nation of priests, destined to bring
praises to God, is made up of both Jew and Gentile.
The two groups, so inexorably opposed in former
times, have been made one through the blood of
Jesus, and together we stand before the Father to
praise His holy name.

The sacrifices we offer up are not the blood of
bulls and goats. Jesus paid the price for our salvation once and for all with His own blood. Our sacrifices are *"sacrifices of praise," "the fruit of our lips."*
We give Him thanks, for He is worthy of all praise!
Our first responsibility as priests of God is to praise
Him, to worship Him, to bless His name!

Just as the key to the prophetic anointing is association with people that have experienced it — find-
ing *"the hill of God"* and associating with *"a company of prophets"* gathered there — the way to obtain the priestly anointing is to spend time with
the Lord, ministering unto Him, worshiping Him.
While we can obtain a prophetic anointing by being around prophetic people, people cannot give
us the priestly anointing. It can only be received in
the very presence of God.

As we obey God in this priestly service, waiting
upon Him, giving Him praise, something wonder-

ful happens. A greater anointing comes upon us, and we are moved into deeper waters.

The priestly anointing, I believe, is another step in the progression of fruitfulness that God has in mind for each of us. It is *"more fruit," "waters to the knees," "the ear,"* a deepening and widening of the channels of the river of life God has placed in His people.

I see the priestly anointing manifested through the revelation gifts, for this is an anointing of wisdom and knowledge:

> *But the manifestation of the Spirit is given to every man to profit withal. For to one is given by the Spirit THE WORD OF WISDOM; to another THE WORD OF KNOWLEDGE by the same Spirit; To another faith by the same Spirit; to another the gifts of healing by the same Spirit; To another the working of miracles; to another prophecy; to another DISCERNING OF SPIRITS; to another divers kinds of tongues; to another the interpretation of tongues: But all these worketh that one and the selfsame Spirit, dividing to every man severally as he will.*
>
> 1 Corinthians 12:7-11

Through ministering unto the Lord, through offering Him our praises, we begin to tap into His endless supply of wisdom and knowledge. We can see this illustrated in the man Simeon:

> *Now, there was a man in Jerusalem called Simeon, who was righteous and devout. He was waiting for the consolation of Israel, and the Holy Spirit was upon him. It had been revealed to him by the Holy Spirit that he would not die before he had seen the Lord's Christ. Moved by the Spirit, he went into the temple courts. When the parents brought in the child Jesus to do for him what the custom and the Law required, Simeon took Him in his arms and praised God, saying:*
>
> *Sovereign Lord, as you have promised,*
> *you now dismiss your servant in peace.*
> *For my eyes have seen your salvation,*
> *which you have prepared in the sight of all people,*
> *a light for revelation to the Gentiles*
> *and for glory to your people Israel.*
>
> Luke 2:25-32, NIV

Simeon was *"waiting"* upon the Lord. Waiting upon the Lord, basking in His presence, brings a greater anointing upon our lives, and that greater flow of the Spirit of God is an anointing of revelation.

Just as Simeon received revelation from God through his priestly anointing — the anointing of revelation — the priestly anointing is the privilege of every believer in the Body of Christ. Since we are all priests of the Lord, His holy nation, His peculiar people, He desires that we have revelation knowledge of the Word of God and the Spirit of wisdom and revelation in us.

The Apostle Paul, in writing to the Ephesians, encouraged them to contend for a greater anointing. While he rejoiced in the spiritual progress they had made, he prayed much for them, because there was much more for them to receive:

> *Wherefore I also, after I heard of your faith in the Lord Jesus, and love unto all the saints, Cease not to give thanks for you, making mention of you in my prayers.* Ephesians 1:15-16

Some might wonder why Paul was praying so hard for the Ephesians. They had been born again and spirit-filled. We know that from the historical account of the book of Acts. The Ephesians had already received the *"waters to the ankles,"* and were flowing in the prophetic anointing. What was the greater level of anointing, then, that Paul desired for them? What was the greater glory to which he felt they should aspire?

Those questions are answered by the continuation of his prayer for them, and we can easily see what he was asking God to do for them:

The Priestly Anointing

*That the God of our Lord Jesus Christ, the Father
of glory, may give unto you the spirit of wisdom
and revelation in the knowledge of Him.*

Ephesians 1:17

*"The spirit of wisdom and revelation in the knowl-
edge of Him"* — this was the new anointing that
Paul felt was so important to the Ephesian believers that he prayed without ceasing for them. This
is what he considered to be another degree of glory
they should seek. And God was speaking through
Paul, which shows us that God wants to give *"the
spirit of wisdom and revelation in the knowledge of Him"*
to every member of the Body of Christ.

It is possible to be saved and spirit-filled and still
not have *"the spirit of wisdom and revelation in the
knowledge of Him."* While God is all wisdom and
knowledge, that wisdom and knowledge does not
automatically transfer to us when we are saved. We
must get closer to God, wait on Him, minister to
Him, and show our desire before He intrusts the
riches of His wisdom to us. Although the Ephesians
had received the prophetic anointing, they had yet
to receive the priestly anointing. And Paul felt it
was important for them to seek it.

As Paul continues his prayer, we can see what
the results would be of such a mantle upon the Ephesians:

The eyes of your understanding being enlight-
ened; that ye may know what is the hope of his
calling, and what the riches of the glory of his
inheritance in the saints.   Ephesians 1:18

God has a greater revelation for each of us con-
cerning our place in Christ, the glory that is our
inheritance, and exactly what is possible to us because we are called to be the sons of God. Many
Christians have never received that revelation and
are ignorant of their true potential, because they
have never learned to flow in the priestly anointing of revelation.

There are many reasons: Some Christians attend
churches where seeking a greater anointing is not
encouraged or even permitted. Other Christians
may indeed come into contact with the prophetic
anointing, and may themselves speak with tongues
and prophesy, but when they leave the house of
the Lord, they don't continue to spend time with
God, waiting in His presence, and ministering unto
Him. Being with the Lord is the key to the priestly
anointing, and there is no substitute. Simeon was
waiting upon the Lord when a great revelation
came to him, and you and I must do the same.

Another example can be found in the historical
account of developments in the early church in
Antioch:

The Priestly Anointing

Now there were in the church that was at Anti-och certain prophets and teachers; as Barnabas, and Simeon that was called Niger, and Lucius of Cyrene, and Manaen, which had been brought up with Herod the tetrarch, and Saul. As they ministered to the Lord, and fasted, the Holy Ghost said, Separate me Barnabas and Saul for the work whereunto I have called them. And when they had fasted and prayed, and laid their hands on them, they sent them away.   Acts 13:1-3

We notice here, again, the presence of recognized leaders in the church, *"prophets and teachers,"* offic-ers who had a specific function within the Body of Christ. They were laying hands upon people, prophesying over them, and sending them forth into their divine callings, to fulfill their God-given destinies.

But even this group of men found it necessary to wait on the Lord, to worship Him, to minister unto Him. They needed wisdom to govern well, and that wisdom only comes from above. Only by spending time in God's presence could these leaders have the spirit of revelation they needed to fulfill their assigned duties.

Just as it always does, this principle of getting close to God in order to feel His heartbeat, in order to know His ways, in order to hear clearly His voice, worked for the men of Antioch. As they worshiped

65

the Lord, clear guidance came to them, a word that was to affect great parts of the world, as Barnabas and Paul were sent forth to present the Gospel of Christ in many other parts of the known world.

In Old Testament times, the people of Israel took care of their priests so that the priests could spend their time in the Temple. The Israelites understood that if they were to receive the wisdom and revelation they needed to overcome their enemies and remain strong and prosperous, they must hear regularly from God. The priests, therefore, lived near or in the Temple and spent a great part of their time before its altars, waiting upon the Lord, exalting His name, seeking His face for the people.

The incense, which was a symbol of the worship of God's people coming up before Him, was kept burning at all times. In fact, certain priests were assigned the responsibility of making sure that it never stopped burning. This speaks to us of continual ministry before the Lord, ministry which brings us into a new anointing, an anointing of revelation.

Jesus showed us that it was not enough to have *"the blade."* That was only a first step. We must go on to the development of *"the corn,"* then persist until we see *"the full corn in the ear,"* or our greatest possible degree of productivity.

When we function in the prophetic anointing, God is pleased. We are bringing forth *"fruit."* But

The Priestly Anointing

He wants us to bring forth *"more fruit,"* to move into a higher anointing, to receive a new surge of power, the priestly anointing, revelation knowledge that will flow into us from the mind of God and will cause us to become more fruitful in His Kingdom. And there will be more to come, for God desires *"much fruit"* from His people."

First the blade ... then the ear ... then the full corn in the ear.

Fruit ... then *more fruit ...* then *much fruit.*

The waters to the ankles ... then *waters to the knees ...* then *waters to the loins.*

God has an endless supply of blessing for us. Take a second step.

The Apostle Paul wrote:

> *But as it is written, Eye hath not seen, nor ear heard, neither have entered into the heart of man, the things which God hath prepared for them that love him. But God hath revealed them unto us by his Spirit: for the Spirit searcheth all things, yea, the deep things of God. For what man knoweth the things of a man, save the spirit of man which is in him? even so the things of God knoweth no man, but the Spirit of God.*
>
> *Now we have received, not the spirit of the world, but the spirit which is of God; that we might know the things that are freely given to us of God. Which things also we speak, not in the words*

which man's wisdom teacheth, but which the Holy Ghost teacheth; comparing spiritual things with spiritual. But the natural man receiveth not the things of the Spirit of God: for they are foolishness unto him: neither can he know them, because they are spiritually discerned. But he that is spiritual judgeth all things, yet he himself is judged of no man. For who hath known the mind of the Lord, that he may instruct him? But we have the mind of Christ.   1 Corinthians 2:9-16

"We have the mind of Christ." What does that mean? It means that we know what Christ knows. We feel what He feels. We sense what He senses. How wonderful! To have the mind of Christ is to have revelation knowledge, to know what He knows about any particular situation we may face. This is a great privilege.

Because we are priests of the Lord and because we are waiting upon Him and ministering unto Him, because we are offering up sacrifices of praise to Him continually, spending time with Him in private, worshiping Him, He opens His heart to us and shares His vast knowledge and wisdom with us. This is the priestly anointing.

In the Sermon on the Mount, Jesus suggested that we might want to enter into a closet to pray, and that, once inside, we might want to shut the door. Some have wondered why that was so important.

The Priestly Anointing

It is important because, by shutting the door, we are shutting out all distractions. We want to give God our full and undivided attention. We need to hear from Him, and we want to hear clearly what He is saying to us. So we shut the door.

In our modern world, with its busyness and its many voices calling to us, closing the door is more important than ever before. If we are to see God cut out the deeper channels among the rocks of our souls, if we are to see Him widen the river bed and release a greater flow of anointing and power in our lives, we must spend more time with Him.

Waiting upon the Lord and ministering to Him must be done on a daily basis. This is not a Sundays-only requirement. We need God every day of our lives. We need His wisdom for every decision. We need His guidance to face every situation. Seek His face regularly.

When we learn to wait upon the Lord, to give Him time regularly, it isn't long before we begin to sense that the water is rising, that the level of anointing in our lives is increasing. This only quickens our desire for Him, causing us to spend even more time with Him. And the more time we spend in His presence, the more revelation knowledge and wisdom will flow into our lives. Before long, we will have a more full and complete comprehension of who we are in Christ and who He is in us.

Paul's prayer for the Ephesians was not unique. He prayed a similar prayer for the Corinthians:

*For this cause we also, since the day we heard it,
do not cease to pray for you, and to desire that ye
might be filled with the knowledge of His will in
all wisdom and spiritual understanding.*

1 Corinthians 2:9-16

Paul was a busy man, yet he took time to pray
daily for the spirit of revelation to come to his
Corinthian brothers, that they would move forward
into greater fruitfulness, into the priestly anointing. *"Filled with the knowledge of His will in all wisdom and spiritual understanding."* This is God's will
for every single one of us.

This word *filled* is translated from the Greek word
pleruo and means *to be crammed full or made replete,
to have no more need.* It is the same word used in
Acts 2:4, when it says:

*And they were all FILLED with the Holy Ghost,
and began to speak with other tongues ... .*

They were *crammed full, made replete and had no
more need.*

This is also the same word translated *"supply"* in
Philippians 4:19, where it says:

*But my God shall supply all of your need accord-
ing to His riches and glory by Christ Jesus.*

The Priestly Anointing

So, in the material sense, God has promised to *cram full and make replete until you have no more need*, according to His divine abilities. This is a wonderful word.

In Romans 10:12, this same word *pleruo* is translated *"rich"*:

> *For there is no difference between the Jew and the Greek: for the same Lord is RICH unto all that call upon Him.*

God is no respecter of persons. He has promised to *cram full, make replete, until he have no more need* every man who comes to Him, regardless of background. Since riches of all types come from God, it makes no difference who we are, but Who He is.

God's perfect will for you is that you be *crammed full, made replete and have no more need* — spiritually, physically, and emotionally. But this comes only as you get tuned in to the river, only as you learn to wait upon God and fellowship and commune with Him in the Spirit, only as you worship Him *"in spirit and in truth."*

Paul prayed the exact same prayer for the Colossians, as well:

> *That ye might walk worthy of the Lord unto all pleasing, being fruitful in every good work, and increasing in the knowledge of God. Strength-*

71

*ened with all might, according to His glorious
power, unto all patience and long suffering with
joyfulness. Giving thanks unto the Father, which
hath made us meet to be partakers of the inheritance of the saints in light: Who hath delivered us
from the power of darkness, and hath translated
us into the kingdom of his dear son.*

Colossians 1:10-13

This is the key to a productive life, to success in
every Christian endeavor. God has promised that
everything we put our hands to would prosper: *"being fruitful in every good work."* This happens only as
we wait upon God and are filled with the knowledge of His will, only as we learn to live a life pleasing Him. Then we become productive in every good
work and constantly increase in the knowledge of
God.

This is, in no way, the common experience of the
average believer in the Body of Christ today, for
many have never learned to wait upon the Lord
and to tap into His resources. Relatively few have
moved into the priestly anointing and begun to
prosper through the revelation knowledge from
above.

The priestly anointing brings us innumerable
benefits and blessings. Among them are the ability
to endure under all circumstances because we have
"all patience and longsuffering with joyfulness." The

priestly anointing causes us to rejoice in every circumstance of life, for we know that we have a great inheritance in God and that, most of all, we are spiritually sound, having been delivered from Satan's kingdom and translated into God's Kingdom.

Jesus was the Son of God, yet He spent time in the Father's presence, at times, praying all night long. When the Pharisees questioned Him about how He did His mighty works, He was able to answer them:

> *My Father worketh hitherto, and I work. ... Verily, verily, I say unto you, The Son can do nothing of himself, but what he seeth the Father do: for what things soever he doeth, these also doeth the Son likewise. For the Father loveth the Son, and sheweth him all things that himself doeth: and he will shew him greater works than these, that ye may marvel.* John 5:17-20

Because Jesus came to Earth as a man, He willingly accepted the limits that required. The works He did were done only because He learned to spend time with the Father, to give glory to the Father and to enter into the priestly anointing. The result was revelation knowledge in His life. And because He knew the Father's heart, He could do the things the Father was doing. In the very same way, God has allowed you and I to participate in His glory.

His anointing that comes upon us enables us to do His works, through the operation of the gifts of the Spirit in our lives.

We can think what God is thinking; we can say what God is saying; and we can do what God is doing. We have *"the mind of Christ,"* through the priestly anointing.

Having *"the mind of Christ"* represents a great mystery. Through His presence in our lives, we become one with God, not just theoretically, but experientially. This gives Him the liberty to cut out rivers among the rocks of our lives.

Paul wrote:

> *He that is joined to the Lord is one spirit.*
> 1 Corinthians 6:17

What a wonderful mystery! And you can experience it.

Are you willing to associate with people who flow in prophetic ministry? Are you willing to find *"the hill of God"* and be a part of *"the company of prophets"*? Are you willing to wait upon the Lord and spend time with Him, ministering praises unto His name? If you will spend time with the Lord regularly, staying in His presence and communing with Him through the Holy Spirit, He will begin to impart grace to you. The Bible shows us:

The Priestly Anointing

Likewise, ye younger, submit yourselves unto the elder. Yea, all of you be subject one to another, and be clothed with humility: for God resisteth the proud, and GIVETH GRACE TO THE HUMBLE.
1 Peter 5:5

You will receive gifts of revelation, gifts of understanding and knowledge, and *"The eyes of your understanding"* will be *"enlightened"* as you move into your priestly anointing. In fact, there is no limit to what you can receive in this way:

For the LORD God is a sun and shield: the LORD will give grace and glory: no good thing will he withhold from them that walk uprightly.
Psalm 84:11

Let us learn to wait upon God in daily prayer and communion and fellowship because it is through such time spent in His presence that He cuts out the rivers, widening and deepening the channel through which His power can flow in our lives. Move on in. The waters are *"TO THE KNEES."*

CHAPTER FOUR

THE KINGLY ANOINTING

*A*gain he measured a thousand, and
brought me through; the waters were TO
THE LOINS.   Ezekiel 47:4

The level of anointing upon our lives increases
as we allow the Lord to carve out rivers among the
rocks of our souls, and we move from the first level
of anointing, the prophetic anointing, to the second level, the priestly anointing. And when we have
risen to those spiritual heights, we are ready to
move into yet another anointing. First *"to the
ankles,"* then *"to the knees,"* and now we are ready
for waters *"to the loins."* This, I believe, is where
the Church of Jesus Christ finds itself today.

In the restoration movement of the last twenty-
five years, we have seen the Church begin to flow
mightily in the prophetic anointing. Believers have

grown accustomed to gathering together, laying hands on one another and prophesying over each other, speaking forth a word of edification, exhortation and comfort.

We have also seen the manifestation of priestly anointing in the Body as revelation knowledge has begun to flow to those who yield themselves to God through the priestly ministry of worship in His presence. Spirit-filled believers have learned to wait upon the Lord more, to honor His presence, and to allow Him to reveal His wisdom and knowledge to His people. But there is more — much more.

The Apostle Paul wrote to his spiritual children in Thessalonica:

> *Night and day we pray most earnestly that we may see you again and supply what is lacking in your faith.*　　　1 Thessalonians 3:10, NIV

Paul had a strong desire to visit the Thessalonians so that he could bring them to a higher level in their spiritual life. He wanted to teach them who they were in Christ and who Christ was in them. If they could be taught the deeper truths of the Word, he knew, they could rise to a greater level of anointing. Their progress was limited only by their lack of understanding of the power that lay within them.

This is the exciting thing about our God: He always has something new and better for us. In the prophetic anointing, we find our voice and speak forth words of encouragement. In the priestly anointing we have the word of knowledge, the word of wisdom and discerning of spirits, and God reveals things to us by His Spirit. But, once we have experienced these two levels of anointing, it is time to move on to greater things. This is the challenge facing the Church today.

The next level of anointing that we must receive, corporately and individually, is the kingly anointing. Just as we have been made prophets and priests unto God, He has made us kings, as well.

He hath made us KINGS and priests unto God.
Revelation 1:6

It is time to accept the kingly anointing and to manifest it to the world.

What is this kingly anointing? The kingly anointing is the power of God at work in us and through us. It enables us to *"work the works of [God]."* Jesus said:

I must work the works of him that sent me, while it is day: the night cometh, when no man can work. John 9:4

The wonderful thing is that He said we could also do those works:

Verily, verily, I say unto you, He that believeth on me, the works that I do shall he do also; and greater works than these shall he do; because I go unto my Father. And whatsoever ye shall ask in my name, that will I do, that the Father may be glorified in the Son.　　　John 14:12-14

Jesus promised, in no uncertain terms, that we could come to the place spiritually that we could do the same works He did. He did mighty works because He was the King of kings, and we can do mighty works because we have been made kings unto God.

As a man, Jesus showed us what is possible when we are anointed of the Father:

The spirit of the Lord God is upon me, because he hath anointed me to preach the gospel to the poor; he hath sent me to heal the brokenhearted, to preach deliverance to the captives, and recovering of sight to the blind, to set at liberty them that are bruised.　　　Luke 4:18

How God anointed Jesus of Nazareth with the Holy Ghost and with power and went about doing good and healing all that were oppressed of the devil.　　　Acts 10:38

And we can have the same power working in

our lives through the kingly anointing God wants to place upon us.

Three of the gifts of the Spirit are known as gifts of power and represent, to my way of thinking, the kingly anointing:

> *But the manifestation of the Spirit is given to every man to profit withal. For to one is given by the Spirit the word of wisdom; to another the word of knowledge by the same Spirit; To another FAITH by the same Spirit; to another THE GIFTS OF HEALING by the same Spirit; To another THE WORKING OF MIRACLES; to another prophecy; to another discerning of spirits; to another divers kinds of tongues; to another the interpretation of tongues: But all these worketh that one and the selfsame Spirit, dividing to every man severally as he will.*
>
> 1 Corinthians 12:7-11

These gifts enable us to do *"the works of God,"* to be one with Him, not only in word and in thought, but in deed. When we have the kingly anointing, we operate in supernatural faith, heal the sick and work miracles. Signs and wonders follow our lives because the anointing has full control of us.

The manifestation of power is the greatest manifestation of God's anointing, and as we reach this third level of anointing in these last days, *"waters to the loins,"* we will be moving in the fullness of all that God has for us. We will be doing the same works that Jesus performed. It is no secret what He did:

> *And it came to pass, when Jesus had made an end of commanding his twelve disciples, he departed thence to teach and to preach in their cities. Now when John had heard in the prison the works of Christ, he sent two of his disciples, And said unto him, Art thou he that should come, or do we look for another? Jesus answered and said unto them, Go and shew John again those things which ye do hear and see: THE BLIND RECEIVE THEIR SIGHT, AND THE LAME WALK, THE LEPERS ARE CLEANSED, AND THE DEAF HEAR, THE DEAD ARE RAISED UP, AND THE POOR HAVE THE GOSPEL PREACHED TO THEM.*   Matthew 11:1-5

Jesus gave sight to the blind, caused the lame to walk, cleansed the lepers, made the deaf to hear and raised the dead. And He said that we would do the same works. These are the fruits of the kingly anointing.

Jesus was anointed to *"destroy the works of the devil"*:

The Kingly Anointing

For this purpose the Son of God was manifested,
that he might destroy the works of the devil.

1 John 3:8

We can do this same ministry of destroying Satan's works — through the kingly anointing. We don't have to wring our hands about the problems of fear and poverty and moral decay that are destroying our society. Through the power gifts of the Holy Ghost, we can open prison doors for *"them that are bound."* We are anointed to *"set at liberty them that are bruised."* We can bring deliverance to suffering humanity, and we must.

Saul was anointed to be king of Israel by the prophet Samuel. One day, when word reached Saul that pagan armies were approaching and threatening the security of his people, the Spirit of God moved upon him, and he rose up in kingly power to destroy the works of the enemy. It is an interesting story:

Then Nahash the Ammonite came up, and encamped against Jabeshgilead: and all the men of Jabesh said unto Nahash, Make a covenant with us, and we will serve thee.
And Nahash the Ammonite answered them, On this condition will I make a covenant with you, that I may thrust out all your right eyes, and lay it for a reproach upon all Israel. And the elders

*of Jabesh said unto him, Give us seven days' res-
pite, that we may send messengers unto all the
coasts of Israel: and then, if there be no man to
save us, we will come out to thee.*

*Then came the messengers to Gibeah of Saul, and
told the tidings in the ears of the people: and all
the people lifted up their voices, and wept. And,
behold, Saul came after the herd out of the field;
and Saul said, What aileth the people that they
weep? And they told him the tidings of the men
of Jabesh.*

*And the Spirit of God came upon Saul when he
heard those tidings, and his anger was kindled
greatly. And he took a yoke of oxen, and hewed
them in pieces, and sent them throughout all the
coasts of Israel by the hands of messengers, saying, Whosoever cometh not forth after Saul and
after Samuel, so shall it be done unto his oxen.
And the fear of the LORD fell on the people, and
they came out with one consent. And when he
numbered them in Bezek, the children of Israel
were three hundred thousand, and the men of Ju-
dah thirty thousand.*

*And they said unto the messengers that came,
Thus shall ye say unto the men of Jabeshgilead,
Tomorrow, by that time the sun be hot, ye shall
have help. And the messengers came and shewed
it to the men of Jabesh; and they were glad. Therefore the men of Jabesh said, Tomorrow we will*

come out unto you, and ye shall do with us all that seemeth good unto you.

And it was so on the morrow, that Saul put the people in three companies; and they came into the midst of the host in the morning watch, and slew the Ammonites until the heat of the day: and it came to pass, that they which remained were scattered, so that two of them were not left together.

And the people said unto Samuel, Who is he that said, Shall Saul reign over us? bring the men, that we may put them to death. And Saul said, There shall not a man be put to death this day: for to day the LORD hath wrought salvation in Israel. 1 Samuel 11:1-13

When God's Spirit comes upon us, we can save people from the enemies that threaten them. We can set men and women free. We have been ordained of God for this very purpose.

This anointing that came upon Saul was the same kingly anointing that came upon Jesus and enabled Him to *"destroy the works of the devil,"* and it is the same kingly anointing that comes upon you and me, as believers, for the purpose of tearing down Satan's strongholds in our day.

The judges who were set by God to rule over His people, during the period just prior to the kings, had this same anointing. Samson, one of those judges, performed superhuman feats under the anointing: carrying away the gates of a Philistine city and slaying a thousand enemy men with the jawbone of an ass.

This represents the *"waters to the loins,"* a deepening river of God's power that flows through our innermost beings and out to the world around us. It is the result of God's continual cutting among the rocks in our lives. Let Him do His work.

The key to the kingly anointing is faithfulness and obedience. If we are faithful to use what we have been given, God will always give us more. If, on the other hand, we choose to go our own way and disregard God's will, we may suddenly find ourselves completely powerless.

Sampson had supernatural strength — until he disregarded God's specific word for his life. Then he was just as weak as any other man.

Saul also lost his anointing — through disobedience, presumption and self-will — when he performed sacrifices that were not within his official authority. He had been instructed by the prophet Samuel to wait for him to come and perform the necessary sacrifices, but Saul did not listen to the man of God. Instead, he listened to the people clamoring for sacrifice, stepped into an official function, for which he had not been authorized, and thus disobeyed God. It was the beginning of his downfall:

The Kingly Anointing

And he tarried seven days, according to the set time that Samuel had appointed: but Samuel came not to Gilgal; and the people were scattered from him. And Saul said, Bring hither a burnt offering to me, and peace offerings. And he offered the burnt offering. And it came to pass, that as soon as he had made an end of offering the burnt offering, behold, Samuel came; and Saul went out to meet him, that he might salute him.

And Samuel said, What hast thou done? And Saul said, Because I saw that the people were scattered from me, and that thou camest not within the days appointed, and that the Philistines gathered themselves together at Michmash; Therefore said I, The Philistines will come down now upon me to Gilgal, and I have not made supplication unto the LORD: I forced myself therefore, and offered a burnt offering.

And Samuel said to Saul, Thou hast done foolishly: thou hast not kept the commandment of the LORD thy God, which he commanded thee: for now would the LORD have established thy kingdom upon Israel for ever. But now thy kingdom shall not continue: the LORD hath sought him a man after his own heart, and the LORD hath commanded him to be captain over his people, because thou hast not kept that which the LORD commanded thee.   1 Samuel 13:8-14

After having demonstrated his kingly anointing by destroying the enemies of the Kingdom of God, Saul was now making excuses for his disobedience. His excuses, however, were rejected by God. The anointing comes from God, and if we are unwilling to obey Him, that anointing will be lifted, just as it was from Israel's first king.

A consistent life of faithfulness and obedience qualifies men and women for the kingly anointing, nothing else. Faithfulness to God brings greater degrees of anointing. Turning backward always produces loss. It cannot be any other way.

Each of us has received specific instruction from God regarding our personal lives. Each of us has certain personal convictions, certain unique ideas about how to live the Christian life. This is because God has spoken to us as individuals about what to do and what not to do. It is extremely important that we be faithful to those personal convictions, whether others agree with us or not. If we are faithful to our personal convictions, and if we do not compromise them, but walk faithfully and obediently within the guidelines the heavenly Father has laid down for us personally, it will cause us to go from one degree of glory to another. It will cause us to receive a special mantle for these last days, a kingly anointing. And as we continue to walk in obedience, God will take us from victory to victory.

Let us be faithful, as kings to Almighty God. Let

us be careful to be obedient to His commands. And let us, therefore, expect to see His mighty power at work in our lives. Let us expect to see *"the full corn in the ear"* manifested in us in these last days.

Step in. The waters are *"TO THE LOINS."*

CHAPTER FIVE

PUTTING THE ANOINTING IN THE PROPER PERSPECTIVE

*A*nd he said, So is the kingdom of God, as if a man should cast seed into the ground; And should sleep, and rise night and day, and the seed should spring and grow up, he knoweth not how. For the earth bringeth forth fruit of herself; first the blade, then the ear, and after that the full corn in the ear. But when the fruit is brought forth, immediately he putteth in the sickle, because the harvest is come.

Mark 4:26-29

"First the blade ... then the ear ... and after that the full corn in the ear." "Waters to the ankles ... waters to the knees ... waters to the loins." "Fruit ... more fruit ... much fruit." Experiencing the anointing and the

91

fruits of it in our lives is a progressive experience: childhood, adolescence and adulthood. And as we grow we don't always have a sense of putting the anointing in the proper perspective.

One of the characteristics of babies is that they require constant care and, without having a parent nearby to provide such care, cannot continue to exist. Babies not only need the attention a parent gives — the feeding, clothing, bathing and comforting that are an integral part of any infant's care — but have a psychological need to be near someone. They suffer when they are deprived of this parental presence. Another reason parents must stay near their babies during the initial stages of their development is that babies are utterly helpless and cannot be left unattended for safety's sake.

There are two rather unpleasant characteristics of babies: (1) When babies need something, the only way they can express that need is to cry. (2) Babies make a lot of messes, seemingly at the most inopportune moments.

New Christians are so much like babies. In fact, they are babies, spiritual babies. They need constant care and feeding and comforting. And we have to interpret their cries and clean up the messes they unknowingly make.

In one respect, many of us are still babies when it comes to the anointing. Just as a baby needs to see the parent nearby or it becomes fearful and anxious, we often become dependent on the sense of God's presence, the feeling we get when He is there, and we become anxious if we don't feel that. In fact, many Christians never get to know God beyond the "feeling."

Even the disciples had a problem in this matter of the Lord's physical presence. When Jesus told them that He was preparing to go back to Heaven, to become the Great High Priest of the New Covenant, they were terrified. What would they do without Him? They were totally dependent upon His presence. How could they exist if He left them alone?

Jesus comforted His followers with the promise of *"another comforter":*

And I will pray the father, and he shall give you another Comforter, that he may abide with you forever; even the Spirit of truth; whom the world cannot receive, because it seeth him not neither knoweth him: but ye know him; for he dwelleth with you and shall be in you.   John 14:16-17

To the disciples, the physical presence of Jesus was everything, and they couldn't imagine what life would be like without it. They wanted to see Him with their physical eyes, hear Him with their physical ears and touch Him with their physical hands. What they were not realizing at the moment is that Jesus had always existed, even before He took the form of flesh and became a man, and that He would always exist. Although He would return to the Father, He would be just as real as He had ever been while walking with them in Galilee.

What I am trying to say is that knowing the Lord is not receiving a miracle from Him, or feeling the cool breeze of His presence on your face, or hearing a voice. Jesus is a person, and we must get to know Him as a person. He is just as near and just as real as any earthly parent could be, and He can do for us what no other parent can do — whether we see Him or not — whether we feel His presence or not. He's always there. Always!

As we grow up a little in the natural sense, it doesn't bother us that Mom is in the next room, and we can't see her. We have come to trust her and know that she will not leave us, and we are at peace.

The disciples were troubled by the thought of Jesus going away from them, but they shouldn't have been. He would never leave them, and His going away would only result in greater blessing upon their lives. At that moment, they couldn't seem to understand that fact.

Many believers (if not most), in their immaturity, often have this same reaction when they can't sense the presence of the Lord. If they felt His presence in a certain way once, they expect to experience it that same way every time. And if they don't, they get panicky and wonder if the Lord, for some reason, has left them.

Satan, of course, takes advantage of this immaturity. He uses every opportunity he can to tell us that God doesn't love us anymore, that God is not pleased with us, that God has been grieved and has withdrawn Himself from us, that God no longer cares about our problems.

Satan never attacks us when we are feeling the glory of God's presence. He's too wise for that. Instead, he waits until we are feeling alone and forsaken. Then he tries his best to convince us that it just isn't worth the effort required to serve God and to continue to abide by His Word.

At the same time, God has a purpose for leaving us without the sense of His presence. He is trying to teach us not to be so dependent upon our feelings, to trust Him no matter what we feel.

I believe that we can even become addicted to the feeling we get when the anointing of God comes upon us, so much so that we may actually have withdrawal symptoms, distortion and disillusionment, when God seemingly goes to sleep in the boat.

On one occasion, when Jesus got in a boat with His disciples on the Sea of Galilee, He told them to go to the other side of the lake, then He went to the back of the ship and fell asleep. Before long, a storm arose over the lake, one so severe that it appeared the whole group would perish. The disciples rushed to awaken Jesus, and said to Him, "Master, don't you care that we are all about to die?"

And he was in the hinder part of the ship, asleep on a pillow: and they awake him, and say unto him, Master, carest thou not that we perish?

Mark 4:38

Of course He cared, and He was right there. There was no way they could have perished with Him in the ship. Yet they felt insecure when they couldn't see Him, and when He seemed to be unaware of the danger they faced.

I have found this to be a rather common experience. Jesus speaks a word to us, then He seemingly goes to sleep and leaves us to walk by faith in what He has told us. And what do we do? We start wondering if we really heard Him or not, and if we did, where is He now and why is He not with us each step of the way? Are we off course? Are we heading for shipwreck?

It is not uncommon for those who have been believers for many years to still be in this initial stage of development, totally addicted to the need to feel God's presence. Seemingly strong Christians actually go into a depression when God seems to have left them alone for a moment. I experienced it myself.

96

Putting the Anointing In the Proper Perspective

In 1980 my wife Rebecca and I moved to Fairmont, West Virginia, and began to pastor a small church in that town of twenty thousand people. God honored our efforts. Eight years later, our work was prospering, God was moving in our small town, and we had experienced significant numerical growth in our church.

In every service, people were being saved, healed and filled with the power of God. There were times when we never got around to preaching the sermon because the presence of God was so real, and people were being blessed in the altars. It was glorious!

We had also planted some other churches around the state and taken missions trips to several other countries.

I suppose it is natural, at times like that, to feel like you have a special relationship with God and have a "handle" on what He is doing. It may be easy, under those circumstances, to make the big mistake of thinking that you must be very mature because of the way God is working in your midst. What we fail to realize is that Father God is just allowing "the kids" to play with the good things He has given us.

My wife once made a good observation regarding this idea of mistaking "gifts" in the life of a believer for "spiritual maturity." She said, "As pastors, looking for help in a growing church, it is dangerous to employ either staff or volunteers on the basis of 'spiritual experience' and not 'spiritual maturity.' It is good for us all to have proven character before being given responsibility in the local church, where what we do can affect the lives of other people." It's true.

In August of 1988, God sent a special lady with a strong prophetic mantle our way. She was Dr. Lois Burkett, and God sent her to speak a word that would thrust our body into a new phase of God's work in our personal lives and in our ministry to the community and the world.

Through this anointed woman, God said to us that He would teach us many new things because none of the old ways of doing things would work anymore. Over the next several years, this prophecy would be played out as some unusual things began to happen to us.

Soon after Dr. Burkett's meetings with us, I was invited to speak to a conference of Pentecostal churches in the southern part of our state. I was very excited about this invitation and was sure that God would work in the meetings and do some of the great things He had been doing for us at home.

On the first night of the conference, the sanctuary of the church was filled, and the overflow rooms had to be opened. There was a wonderful anointing present. In fact, I can't think of another time I enjoyed more liberty in preaching. The prophetic flow of fresh revelation was amazing. I was very excited about what happened that opening night and thought to myself, "This is going to be some week!"

The next night the church was filled even more than the first night. Many preachers were seated on the front row. They had come to see what was happening in my life. I was determined not to disappoint them. It was my first time to speak in such a conference, and I wanted to do well.

What happened that night, however, was the worst of all nightmares, from my perspective at least. For some unknown and inexplicable reason, there seemed to be absolutely no anointing upon the service. I went through the paces, trying to preach and to pray for people, but nothing was happening, and I didn't know why.

After the service had ended, I could sense that those present were disappointed, and I couldn't blame them. I was disappointed myself. I wasn't sure what had happened, but I was determined that the next night would be as glorious as the first, and I spent time in prayer, preparing for that glory to come.

To my utter dismay, the next night was as dead as the last, and the rest of the week was a disappointment, as well.

I went home from that conference embarrassed and hurt, wondering if I was out of God's will completely and even wondering if I needed a change of vocation. What could have gone wrong? After all, we had been enjoying the mighty presence of God for years in our ministry. Why would that suddenly change?

The next day, when I got home, I got serious with God in prayer, and He began to speak to me in a way I had never known before. For the first time in my life, I felt like I was communing with God face to face, and it continued in this intensity for several days.

During that time God told me that His glory had never been taken from me, but that each phase through which I was passing had a purpose in my spiritual development. He assured me that He was always with me — whether I felt His presence or not — and that I should trust Him to work in my life and ministry.

Ironically, I was tested on this new revelation very quickly. After only a few days of this type of heavenly visitation in my prayer times, the heavens suddenly fell silent. For a period of time, I didn't sense God's presence in my prayer times or in my preaching ministry. I continued as before, trying to "work it up" and "pray it down," but nothing seemed to be working.

When this happened, I remembered the prophecy of Dr. Burkett. It was true. Doing things in the same old way was not producing the same results now. I found the experience very troubling. What was I to do?

I tried increasing my prayer time, praying two hours a day instead of one. I fasted and spent long hours in the Word. I was doing everything I could think of to try to woo God's presence back into my life. Yet nothing seemed to be working.

One morning, at about 5:00 am, I was awakened by my wife moving about in our bedroom. As soon as I got awake, and even before I had a chance to move, God spoke to me in a powerful way. He said, "My people have a relationship with Me on three levels — body, soul and spirit. Many of My people only come to Me when they need something, such as healing for their bodies or financial help. Others, who are soulish believers, come to Me only when they need to feel My presence and have their joy and peace renewed. But I want My people to become spiritual people."

Then the Lord quoted Matthew 4:4 to me. It says:

Man shall not live by bread alone, but by every Word that proceedeth out of the mouth of God.

But He quoted this verse to me a little differently. He said: "Man shall live to hear My Voice." I then realized that I had not been living by the Word of God, even though I considered myself to be a "faith preacher." I had been living by the feeling of the anointing, the feeling of the presence of God in my life, not by the Word. When I felt the anointing, I was okay and "had the victory," but when the anointing was not manifest, when I couldn't feel it, I was in fear and doubt. God showed me that a truly spiritual person is not one who feels great anointing, but one who lives to "hear [God's] voice" every day.

This revelation brought such a release to my life that I was quickly on the road to recovery from the emotional tailspin that had overtaken me. After all, there was nothing "wrong" with me. I had not sinned or grieved the Spirit. God was trying to bring me from spiritual infancy to the next phase of my spiritual development.

The thought of having been in "infancy" for eight years, as a pastor, while preaching on radio and television and in crusades in foreign lands, was not a very pleasant one; but I had to admit it was true in many ways. And I was determined to move on to greater things.

I see a parallel in the experience of the Church in the twentieth century. Beginning with the outpouring of the Holy Spirit at the turn of the century, an outpouring that gave us classical Pentecost, the church was reintroduced to the presence and power of the Spirit of God, and went on to bask in copious outpourings under the great ministries of the early 1900s through the late 50s. Too many times, however, the emphasis in these ministries was on an emotional experience. The experience was glorified, and not the Lord Himself. This contributed to a lack of maturity on the part of many believers.

As a Pentecostal preacher myself, I believe in the supernatural as put forth by Scripture and demonstrated throughout church history. I have come to understand, however, that God is much more than "power and demonstration." Power and demonstration is what He does, not what He is. He is a wonderful Person, a Person we should come to know intimately. He is searching for those who will not only follow the signs, but will hear His voice and live by what they hear. It is time to leave the childish aspects of our faith behind, to get into the Word and to learn the principles laid down by our God.

After the great Pentecostal revival, God sent us a "teaching revival." "Knowledge" was the key word of the movement that resulted. A favorite passage was this:

> *My people are destroyed for the lack of knowledge.*
> Hosea 4:6

Great prophetic teachers began to unveil the mysteries of the Word and to bring us the revelation knowledge of who we are in Christ. This

brought with it a renewed faith. I personally re-
member the late 70s and 80s as a time of infusion of
truth into our spirits until we as the Church could
quote the Scriptures and stand upon them.

We now understood what Christ did for us and
how to appropriate it. We now understood that we
had a good God who wasn't killing us in car wrecks
and starving our children to death just to teach us
humility. In fact, the opposite was true. God was
teaching us how to *"prosper and be in health."* These
new biblical concepts attracted many more unsaved
people to come into the church and be saved.

However, even this infusion of knowledge about
God and His work in Christ left us short of what
God was really after; for now we were like a group
of adolescents, experimenting with independence
from their parents. We were sure that we knew
what to do, and we were going to do it on our own
terms, no matter what.

As is so often the result of adolescents gaining
knowledge, we became determined to "do our own
thing," without realizing that the Christian life is
not just independently operating a set of godly principles, it is *"Christ in us."* By demonstrating independence from one another, we were actually as-
serting our independence from God and, aside from
Him, we can bear no fruit.

We felt that we were doing what the Bible says
to do, that we were operating principles that could

not fail, but we were mistaken. And yet we couldn't figure out why it wasn't working as we thought it should.

Knowing principles and knowing God is something very different. We can do things sometimes in the name of the Lord, when, in reality, He has nothing to do with it. We are controlling everything ourselves, and just using His name in the process.

When things did not go as we imagined they should, some were offended and gave up. Others turned back completely.

Adolescence is a dangerous period in our lives, and what we do during that period may determine our paths for many years to come.

When an adolescent nears the end of this most dangerous stage of his life and is approaching maturity, he is often found returning to parents and saying, "I'm ready to take your advice. I admit that I don't know it all." This is a BIG STEP! Humility is the hallmark of maturity, and becoming an adult is more than having an experience or gaining knowledge. It is the realization that you can't make it on your own, that you need the help of God and your fellowman.

When we have taken this big step and entered into the realm of maturity, we will stop saying, "It isn't working," and start saying, instead, "He is working." That's what happened to us.

When our fellowship in Fairmont had outgrown our old building, those of us in leadership decided to buy a large warehouse. We would build a sanctuary inside it, raising the money as we went, and doing the work ourselves, to keep the cost down. We were all sure that God had directed us to buy the building, and we had faith that He would enable us to make the payments.

The owner of the building had been very generous with us, agreeing to hold the mortgage himself. The contract we signed stipulated that we would make no payments for the first year. At the end of that first year, a rather large interest payment was due. And from then on, we would make regular payments on the property until it was paid off.

When we held our first services in the building, we had no ceiling yet and no heat, but we were happy and God was helping us to continue the remodelling program.

When we had taken on the project, we had expected that the numerical growth in our congregation would allow us not only to build and pay cash as we went, but to save enough to make the interest payment at the end of the year. When, after six months, we had nothing at all saved toward the interest payment, I began to get concerned. We had been praying, speaking the Word, and sowing seed. What was wrong? Why wasn't God helping us? I sought Him very seriously about this matter; but, mysteriously, I got no answer at all.

Now, I was a little alarmed. I prayed even harder, fasted and called upon others to help us in the battle we were facing against defeat. How could we risk losing this facility God had so miraculously given to us for His glory?

Without realizing it, I began developing a resentment toward the congregation for not giving more. After all, my family was leading by example. We were sowing the largest seeds into the building fund. Someone had to help us! And quickly!

But no help came.

When the agreed-upon year had passed and the day arrived that the large interest payment was due, we had nothing at all toward it. I was rather numb at the thought. Could we risk default? Could we allow God's name to be dragged through the mud because we couldn't meet our commitments? What exactly could we do? I had no idea.

When I got to the office that day, a secretary handed me a phone message. It was from the man who owned the building. I knew what he wanted, but what could I say to him?

I held the note up to Heaven and said, "Do you see this, God?"

I'm not sure if I was expecting an immediate answer or not. For a whole year the Lord had been silent on this issue, not answering me when I pleaded for an answer. But this day was to be different. "Ask the man what he can do about it," the Lord said to me.

I couldn't believe what I was hearing. In effect, the Lord was telling me to ask the owner how *he* could pay himself the interest payment. That sounded crazy to me. But I felt encouraged that God was speaking to me again, and I went to make the phone call.

I don't know if I managed to sound calm or not, especially when the man asked, "Rev. Polis, do have the interest payment?"

I managed to answer, "No, I don't. What can your people do about it?"

What transpired that day amazed all of us. The man calmly accepted my answer and agreed to incorporate the interest payment into the total loan. Two years later, when he needed money himself, he offered us a debt reduction of several thousand dollars more than that original interest payment if we could find a local bank to take the mortgage and give him his money. We did that and came out on top, saving more than the original interest payment in the process.

God had everything under control from the very first day. He never intended for us to pay that interest payment, and my getting high blood pressure by worrying about it just proved that I didn't know God as I should have. I was frantically working all the principles, while I should have been rest-ing in a Person that I loved and trusted. Reaching adulthood, that most fruitful and productive stage of our Christian life and ministry, is the result of knowing the presence of God, the principles of God and the Person of God.

The Apostle Paul, speaking from an intimate relationship of trust in a Person whom he had learned to know by walking with Him for many years, said:

> *For the which cause I also suffer these things: nevertheless I am not ashamed: for I know whom I have believed, and am persuaded that he is able to keep that which I have committed unto Him against that day.*   2 Timothy 1:12

When we know a person, we know what that person likes and dislikes. We even know what that person thinks and can anticipate their next move. Paul could express this type of confidence in God because He had progressed through the stages of growth and had come to a "face to face" relationship with God where he "lived to hear [God] speak." From prison, toward the end of his life, he could confidently say:

> *I know that the Lord will deliver me from every evil work and preserve me safely to his heavenly kingdom.*   2 Timothy 4:17-18

Living to hear God's Voice implies that we are

not only willing, but eager to do whatever He says.
Jesus said:

> *He that hath my commandments [hears God's voice] and keepeth them, he it is that loveth me: and he that loveth me shall be loved of my father, and I will love him and manifest [reveal] myself to him.* John 14:21

This is where I believe we are in the Church today. We have come to the realization that our supreme quest is not to build an earthly kingdom, but to know Christ. Many modern-day ministers are speaking of the need for intimacy with God and this renewed interest in intimacy has resulted in the Spirit being poured out upon the Church in a new way.

God is raising up a people in these last days who know Him — not just His presence and His principles. Those who press into this relationship God is so generously offering His people have great promise:

> *The people that do know their God shall be strong, and do exploits.* Daniel 11:32

CHAPTER SIX

MOVING INTO DEEPER WATERS

Afterward he measured a thousand; and it was a river that I could not pass over: for the waters were risen, waters to swim in, a river that could not be passed over.

Ezekiel 47:5

For some time now God has been cutting out the rivers among the rocks in our lives. He has been blowing up the dams in our spirits, removing those things which are hindrances and obstructions to the free flow of the anointing through us. Now, He is about to burst forth with a flood of anointing glory that will excel anything we have seen thus far and will bring us into the fullness of His will for us in these final days of time. What an exciting time to be alive!

God is preparing His Church for the coming of

the Lord Jesus Christ, and before He comes, we must be sure that our anointing is complete. That it covers us, even *"to the skirts of [the] garments"*:

> *It is like the precious ointment upon the head,*
> *that ran down upon the beard, even Aaron's beard:*
> *that went down to the skirts of his garments.*
>
> Psalm 133:2

It is no longer enough to be anointed. We need that anointing to cover us fully, to take control of our lives. It is time for a deeper plunge, into the fullness of God's provision. It is time to swim on out into the increasing flow of God's anointing.

I see even now, with the eye of my spirit, the anointing flowing. It comes down from the Master's hand, from the Head of the Church, our Lord Jesus Christ. As this heavy weight of glory flows down over the Body, the Body receives a new infusion of God's grace and a new quickening to manifest His power in the world.

I see segments of the Body which have been covered with the holy anointing oil, being enfolded into the priestly anointing; some are being enfolded into the prophetic anointing; and some are being enfolded into the kingly anointing. It is happening right this very moment.

We are living in times of divine restoration, as the Scriptures promised:

Moving Into Deeper Waters

Repent ye therefore, and be converted, that your
sins may be blotted out, when the times of re-
freshing shall come from the presence of the Lord;
And he shall send Jesus Christ, which before was
preached unto you: Whom the heaven must re-
ceive until the times of restitution of all things,
which God hath spoken by the mouth of all his
holy prophets since the world began.

Acts 3:19-21

This divine program will bring the complete restoration of all truth, of all gifts, and of all ministries
of the Holy Ghost to the Church, just before the
coming of Jesus. There are three defined steps to
be taken for anyone wanting to participate in what
God is doing today: repent, be refreshed and be re-
stored.

Now is the time. The windows of Heaven are
open, and God is pouring out His Spirit upon hun-
gry hearts. Doors of ministry are opening. Opportunities abound for us to take what we have been
given to the whole world and thus hasten the glorious coming of our Lord Jesus Christ.

There has never been a greater time to be alive.
Walls of separation have come down in country after country, until the whole world has become God's
harvest field. And the Church of the Lord Jesus
Christ is going forth into that harvest field and pro-
claiming the Gospel of the Kingdom to every na-

tion, kindred, tongue and tribe. This is our destiny. This is our prophetic purpose. Rejoice, children of God! And plunge on in to these *"waters."*

Because we are living in the very last days of time, we are entering into a period of the greatest manifestation of God's healing and delivering power that the Church has ever seen. This power will not be for everyone, but for those who have been faithful in little things.

Jesus declared:

> *For whosoever hath, to him shall be given, and he shall have more abundance: but whosoever hath not, from him shall be taken away even that he hath.* Matthew 13:12

Those who have been faithful to flow in their prophetic mantle, shall begin to walk in the priestly anointing. Those who have been faithful to walk in the priestly anointing shall begin to operate in the kingly anointing. And those who are faithful in the kingly anointing will move on out into *"waters to swim in."*

When we move from one level of anointing to another, it doesn't mean that we forsake our previous experience. We don't forsake it, we just add to it, moving out into deeper waters. What are we waiting for?

The signs, wonders and miracles of the end times will be just as glorious and just as awesome as those of the founding period of the Church. The power demonstrated so remarkably in the ministry of Jesus, and later, in the ministry of the apostles, will return in these last days, to all those who have pressed in to *"touch the hem of His garment."*

There is a great difference between being touched by God and reaching out ourselves to touch Him. Many people have been touched by God, meaning that God initiated the move. He reached out to them:

> *For the Son of man is come to seek and to save*
> *that which was lost.*   Luke 19:10

> *For the eyes of the Lord run to and fro through-*
> *out the whole earth, to show himself strong in*
> *behalf of them whose heart is perfect toward Him.*
>   2 Chronicles 16:9

God sovereignly reaches out to man and touches him. On the other hand, it is possible for man to reach out to God. We can do the searching and initiation of contact, reaching out for God, because of the hunger and thirst of our hearts. In David's immortal words:

> *As the hart [deer] panteth after the water brooks,*
> *so panteth my soul after thee, O God.*
>   Psalm 42:1

That panting for the rivers of living water, that panting for the courts of God, for the fragrance of His glory and anointing upon our lives, is that which causes us to press through the crowd (just as the little woman with the issue of blood), against all odds, until we touch Jesus.

When the Scriptures speak of touching God, therefore, this refers to our longing and searching, to our setting ourselves apart from others, and from anything else that might hinder us, and reaching out to Him, pressing in, touching Him in His glory and fullness.

This move toward God must be initiated by the individual believer if we are to touch Him and receive an impartation of His mantle in our lives. And many are receiving today. Swim on out. The *"waters"* are fine.

Are you waiting for God to touch you? Or are you reaching out to touch Him? Are you expecting His touch to enable you to change the world around you?

Jesus changed His world by operating in His kingly anointing and by manifesting the power of God everywhere He went. He was one with the Father — in thought, word and deed — through the gifts of the Holy Ghost. Now, through the prophetic, priestly and kingly anointings, you and I can become one with God the Father. We can speak His word, think His thoughts, and do His works.

This is the "glorious Church" for which Jesus Christ will return.

Jesus had the Spirit without measure:

For he whom God hath sent speaketh the words of God: for God giveth not the Spirit by measure unto him.   John 3:34

I believe it is God's will for the Church to walk in that same unlimited anointing. Christ is the Anointed One and was sent to demonstrate God's power to the world. Now we, as Christians, must be God's anointed ones. We are *"the light of the world," "the salt of the earth,"* God's representatives to our generation.

I am convinced that in these last days we will walk in the fullness of the anointing that Jesus demonstrated while He was here on planet Earth. We will possess the nine fruits of the Spirit and the nine gifts of the Spirit in their full manifestation within the Body of Christ. This is the "glorious church" that will greet Him when He comes, a Church which has fully participated in end-time revival.

What exciting days these are! Is the river of God's anointing flowing in your life? Is it daily cutting a deeper and wider path through which to increase its flow?

As we become one with Jesus in word, through the prophetic anointing, and one with Him in thought, through the priestly anointing, and one with Him in deed, through the kingly anointing, we find that we are only beginning to tap into His wonders. He has prepared for us those *"waters to swim in."* He has much more than we could ever anticipate and He wants to fully envelop us in His glory, until we come to that promised day of which the Scriptures speak:

Till we all come in the unity of the faith, and of the knowledge of the Son of God, unto a perfect man, unto the measure of the stature of the fulness of Christ: Ephesians 4:13

Amen!

INDEX OF SCRIPTURE REFERENCES USED

∽ Notes ∾

⍟ Notes ⍟

❧ Notes ❧

cs **Notes** so

❧ Notes ❧

❧ Notes ❧